Making Choices for Health Care

Making Choices for Health Care

Edited by

Frank Honigsbaum
Stefan Holmström
and
Johan Calltorp

Sponsored by

The University of Birmingham in collaboration
with The Nordic School
of Public Health
and Bure Health Care

Radcliffe Medical Press

Radcliffe Medical Press Ltd
18 Marcham Road, Abingdon, Oxon OX14 1AA, UK

Radcliffe Medical Press, Inc.
141 Fifth Avenue, New York, NY 10010, USA

British Library Cataloguing in Publication Data

A catalogue record for this book is available from the British Library.

ISBN 1 85775 251 1

Library of Congress Cataloging-in-Publication Data is available.

Typeset by Advance Typesetting Ltd, Oxfordshire
Printed and bound by Biddles Ltd, Guildford and King's Lynn

Contents

List of contributors

Sweden:	Johan Calltorp, *Professor of Health Services Management, Nordic School of Public Health*
Oregon:	Tina Castanares, *Former member of the Health Services Commission*
New Zealand:	Wendy Edgar, *Programme Director, Core Services Committee, Ministry of Health*
University of Birmingham:	Chris Ham, *Director and Professor of Health Policy and Management, Health Services Management Centre*
Sweden:	Stefan Holmström, *MD, Bure Health Care (formerly Acting Director at the Department of Community Medicine at Huddinge Hospital and Medical Advisor at the Federation of Swedish County Councils)*

University of Birmingham: Frank Honigsbaum, *Senior Research Fellow, Health Services Management Centre*

The Netherlands: Jannes H. Mulder, *Ministry of Health*

Norway: Kari Rolstad, *Kommunenes Sentralforbund, Norwegian Association of Local Authorities*

Preface

Funding pressures have forced many countries to find ways of setting priorities in health care. The process is replete with difficulties and various methods have been tried. Recognizing that there is much to be learned from sharing experience, Sweden has taken the initiative in sponsoring two international seminars.

The first was held in Stockholm in October 1993, and the major findings were published in book form (Honigsbaum F, Calltorp J, Ham C, Holmström S (1995) *Priority Setting Processes for Healthcare*. Radcliffe Medical Press, Oxford). A second was held in Birmingham in May 1995, and this study is based on the data supplied there.

Five countries participated in the first seminar and a sixth was added for the second. They are: the USA (Oregon), New Zealand, The Netherlands, Norway, Sweden and the United Kingdom. Contributors came from all six countries and their names are listed on pages vii–viii. They supplied the papers on which the seminar was based.

The seminar was held over two days at the Health Services Management Centre, University of Birmingham. The first day consisted of a private seminar with participants from Sweden and the UK. The second day was open to a larger number of UK participants.

The seminar was sponsored by the Health Services Management Centre in collaboration with the Nordic School of Public Health and Bure Health Care. Professor Chris Ham is Director of the Centre, and he organized the meeting together with Professor Johan Calltorp and Dr Stefan Holmström from Sweden. Frank Honigsbaum, a Senior Research Fellow at the Centre, acted as rapporteur, and this report was prepared by him. Thanks are due to Glaxo Wellcome and the Stockholm County Council for help in financing the seminar and to Bure Health Care for help in financing publication of this book.

It is presented in two parts: the first describes the way in which processes have developed in the six countries, with emphasis on the changes which have occurred since the first seminar. The section dealing with Oregon draws not only on the paper submitted by Dr Castanares but on information obtained by Dr Stefan Holmström and Frank Honigsbaum during a visit to the US in the autumn of 1994. It also takes account of recent changes in the Oregon plan as indicated by Paige Sipes-Metzler, the Executive Director of the Oregon Health Services Commission. She and the contributors to the seminar have read the sections pertaining to them and kindly suggested changes and additions. Additional help was provided by Chris Ham, who reviewed the work as a whole and suggested ways in which it could be improved. His aid was invaluable.

The second part identifies the major trends that are evident and discusses the issues arising from them. References to publications and papers relevant to the seminar are listed at the end on pages 117–123.

This report is based on data and views expressed at seminar proceedings but particularly in the second part, it also draws on interpretative judgements made by the rapporteur. For those, he is solely responsible.

Frank Honigsbaum
Stefan Holmström
Johan Calltorp
February 1997

Part 1

Priority setting models: country comparisons

Oregon

Priority setting in Oregon has proceeded by way of the exclusion of services with the aim of defining a basic package of health care.

The plan, initially at least, applies only to the poor under the Medicaid programme run by the states with the aid of the federal government. Eventually, by extending the package to small businesses and others under private insurance, it is hoped that nearly all in Oregon will be covered. Federal approval was required and was given in the form of a five-year demonstration project.

A list was prepared covering the whole of health care in condition/treatment pairs, such as appendicitis/appendectomy. The pairs were ranked in priority order, mainly in terms of their effectiveness and contribution to basic health. This task was carried out by an 11-member commission and the state legislature decided how far down the list it could afford to go.

The plan began operating in February 1994, with 565 out of 696 lines funded. Conditions that have since been added include mental health and chemical dependency, along with care of the elderly, blind and disabled, and children in foster care. This integrated list began operating in January 1995, with 606 out of 745 lines funded. Mental health services are being phased in, but the legislature has yet to set a date for full integration. Applying the priority setting process and the list to chemical dependency services (alcohol and drug addiction care) did not start until April 1995.

After a year of review, a slightly amended list of 744 lines was prepared on 10 February 1995, with 608 funded. Subsequently, the legislature not only restricted access for the poor by tightening eligibility conditions and imposing charges in the form of monthly premium payments, but decided that it could fund only 581 lines, thereby dropping 27 from coverage. This line movement has to be approved by the federal government, but that was expected by January 1996.

Reaction to the plan

It is too soon to make a firm judgement on the Oregon plan, and reactions may change dramatically once the tighter eligibility qualifications and reduced line coverage come into effect. However, so far the plan appears to be acceptable to Medicaid patients, clinicians and the general public.

- For new Medicaid patients, it raises access from 58% to 100% of the poverty level, eliminates assets from the calculation and opens admittance to single or married persons without children. Under normal Medicaid operation, only those with children are covered. However, in addition to the proposed imposition of monthly premium payments, the new eligibility rules deprive access to those with assets (excluding a house or car) of $5000 or more. This could reduce the numbers eligible and make the plan less acceptable on equity grounds.

- For old Medicaid patients below 58% of the poverty level, the services withheld do not unduly restrict the range of medical treatment formerly covered and dental care is added. However, among the 27 lines to be dropped are a number that will be painful to lose. These include surgical treatment for Bell's palsy, surgical treatment for foot deformities, medical treatment for chronic bronchitis, medical treatment for irritable bowel syndrome and other digestive disorders, and surgical removal of a foreign body accidentally left inside a patient during an operation. All would normally be covered by private insurance plans.
- For clinicians, the plan raises pay for Medicaid services from a low level and the legislation enacted provides protection against cuts.
- For the general public, the plan has thus far had no tax implications except for a rise in the cigarette tax.

In support of these findings, enrolment data indicate that the plan has proved popular, with demand for access exceeding expectations. As of June 1995, 123 000 has been added, raising the total enrolment to 375 000 persons.

Only four services not provided seem to have caused concern, being the subject of the most frequent appeal hearings. They are tonsils and adenoids, phimosis/circumcision, uncomplicated hernias and pneumonia due to RSV, a virus. In the first half of 1995, the surgical operations most often denied were breast reduction (7), tonsillectomy/adenoidectomy (5), inguinal hernia (4) and varicose veins (3).

The two main organizations representing Medicaid patients (Oregon Health Action Campaign and Oregon Fair Share) are reported to be satisfied with the services included. An attempt by a journalist to elicit complaints failed to register a significant response, while a survey of

72 doctors found them to be generally in favour of the scheme. All of this could change once the new conditions come into effect.

When the Oregon plan was first proposed, certain advocacy groups thought that it might endanger the health of women and children as, under usual Medicaid rules, which exclude single or married persons without children, they are the main groups covered. These fears have not been realized. The vast majority of newly insured Medicaid beneficiaries are women and children and no claim of injury or damage due to the implementation of the list has been made by any party.

List compared with private insurance

The services now included in the priority list compare favourably with those provided in many private insurance plans. The latter do not usually cover dental or vision care, and limits are placed on drugs as well as services such as physiotherapy. All are freely provided under the Oregon plan. However, among the 27 lines to be dropped from coverage are, as indicated above, a number that would be included in private insurance plans.

Pending problems

These changes make it less certain that a favourable response will continue. The Oregon state government, like the federal government, faces severe financial problems and may have to impose even more cuts in services. During the recent legislative debate, line 565 was suggested as a cut-off point, which would have excluded treatment for a condition as serious as cancer of the gall bladder.

The addition of expensive mental health procedures may cause further cost pressure. All but eight of the 49 lines added for mental health were covered in the integrated list, but four more will be dropped now that the cut-off point is being raised from 608 to 581.

Further restrictions may also be imposed on access, making the plan less open to the poor. Nor is there any prospect of extending it to a wider segment of the population as originally intended. Small businesses have resisted a mandate requiring them to provide a standard benefit package similar to the Medicaid list. Large employers which do offer health insurance can opt out through federal legislation (called ERISA), which gives them the right to self-insure and provide uniform benefits throughout the country.

Aside from the poor, only high-risk individuals are now affected by the plan, and they generally receive a wider range of benefits. However, unlike Medicaid patients, they bear the cost of insurance themselves or, if employed, with the aid of employers. In any case, the plan calls only for the Medicaid list to be extended as a minimum package. The excluded services may always apply only to the poor.

At one time, it was thought that the Oregon plan could not survive if it were confined to the poor. Now, in the present political climate with less compassionate values prevailing, the opposite view prevails.

Nor are other states following Oregon's lead. Some, faced with budget deficits, have considered using the list simply to restrict the services offered under Medicaid without extending access to the poor. Michigan may follow this procedure if, as expected, block grants for Medicaid are made to the states. That will relieve the federal government of any responsibility for Medicaid provision and leave decisions entirely to the states. But rationing is a distasteful concept in America, and other techniques have been employed to relieve state finances.

Priority setting methods employed

There was no attempt at needs assessment before the priority list was prepared. Oregon, like the USA as a whole, has a serious obesity problem, yet the two services relating to obesity were not funded. Decisions were made largely on the basis of effectiveness, and trials relating to obesity procedures have not produced sufficient evidence of effectiveness.

Yet there is no doubt that some people do benefit from treatment, and the need is so pressing that funding could have been forthcoming. This applies particularly to poor people such as those covered by Medicaid. Living on low incomes, they tend to develop eating habits that bring on weight problems and could benefit from nutritional and lifestyle counselling, ranked 660 on the list.

No precise method was employed to assess the number of people affected by each line item or its importance to society. These, along with other values, were raised at community meetings but were not related in any explicit way to the ranking order. Rather, reliance was placed mainly on the judgements of commission members, which meant a large subjective element went into the process. Only after the list was prepared were actuarial cost calculations made that took account of the number of people affected by each line item.

Before the list was implemented, the commission had to revise it five times, but only the three main revisions need to be considered here.

Rankings based on cost-effectiveness

The first attempt was made solely on the basis of cost-effectiveness, using the cost per quality-adjusted life year (QALY) method to set rank order. This produced so many anomalies that it was swiftly abandoned. Not enough data were available to apply this method. The most serious deficiency was in costs and outcomes.

Category ranking of effective treatments

The next attempt relied on a category method of ranking. Instead of trying to deal with hundreds of items as a whole, they were classified into 17 categories (Figure 1), which were ranked according to community importance. Three groupings were employed, making use of the 13 values supplied by community meetings: essential (to basic health care); very important (to society); and important to the individual (interested in such treatment). The commission then applied the groupings to the ranking of categories by means of a consensus process among its members, which allowed scope for individual judgement and discussion.

The next step was to put the condition/treatment pairs into their proper categories and list them in priority order. This was done by means of a formula based on rates of mortality and quality of well-being. Less weight was attached to cost than in the first attempt, so this method was based mainly on the effects of treatment. However, many items were moved out of category to higher or lower rank based on the judgement of the commission.

The process was completed in 1991, but the list was rejected by the federal government because, by including valuations of quality of life, it might have been found to have

Disease oriented	*Rank*	*Health oriented*
Fatal conditions		
Treatment prevents death:		
Full recovery	1	
	2	Maternity care
Residual problems	3	
	4	Preventive care for children
Treatment extends life and quality of life	5	
	6	Reproductive services
Comfort care	7	
	8	Preventive dental care
	9	Adult preventive care (I)
Non-fatal conditions		
Acute condition: Treatment provides full cure	10	
Chronic condition: Single treatment improves quality of life	11	
Acute condition: Treatment achieves partial recovery	12	
Chronic condition: Repeated treatments improve quality of life	13	
Acute, self-limiting condition: Treatment speeds recovery	14	
	15	Infertility
	16	Adult preventive care (II)
Fatal or non-fatal conditions		
Treatments provide minimal or no improvement in length or quality of life	17	

Figure 1: Health Services Commission priorities by category. (Devised by Oregon Health Services Commission, Portland, USA.)

violated the rights of disabled persons under legislation passed in 1990.

Dollars per life saved remained an acceptable criterion, but only if it measured the effectiveness of treatment, not the subsequent quality of life. Thus, a treatment which saved a limb could be placed higher than one which resulted in loss, but no consideration could be given to the fact that the patient was left in a wheelchair.

Pragmatic approach employed

The category method of classification had to be abandoned because quality of life had figured so prominently in the community values employed. In its place, an entirely new method was devised that is unique to Oregon and not conducive to replication. The only data retained dealt with the probability of preventing death, cost of treatment and medical effectiveness.

Priorities were assigned in the following order:

1. Does treatment prevent death?
2. If tied on the first basis, then lower cost pairs were placed above those with higher costs.
3. Community values other than quality of life were then used to change rankings. Prevention was given a higher priority and so was impact on society. Both had been classified as essential for the purpose of preparing the 1991 list. But two values considered only of importance to an individual received more attention in the 1992 list; they were effectiveness of treatment and length of life.
4. Some services were ranked on the basis of specific conditions rather than community values. High rankings were given to comfort care as well as maternity and

family planning services; low rankings went to cosmetic services and self-limiting conditions.

5. Manual adjustments were then made by the commissioners, which produced substantial changes in the ranking order.

Public consultation

In its initial work, the commission drew on public opinion in three ways.

1. Public values, 13 in number, were obtained from community meetings held throughout the state. A total of 1048 people participated in 47 meetings, which meant that the average attendance was only 22. Nor were the meetings truly representative of the public; fewer than 50 were Medicaid recipients, while more than two-thirds of those attending were health workers who provided the services under consideration. Possibly a number came from the mental health sector, which may explain why mental health itself was regarded as a public value.
2. The weights used for measuring quality of life were obtained from a phone survey of 1001 respondents. This was the most important technique employed and was used to elicit weights for quality of life scores. Disabled as well as unaffected people were randomly selected for this survey, but the federal government apparently felt that insufficient weight was given to the views of disabled persons.
3. Hearings were held for the public, and this also provided a means for testimony to be taken from those who received care under Medicaid as well as from those who provided services. Over 1500 people attended

> 12 hearings, with the number testifying ranging from 13 to 62. However, only 280 testimonies were recorded, with the greatest stress being put on the desirability of preventive care and mental health services. The testimony was of a rambling nature, useful only 'for understanding the general tone of public needs and concerns'.[1]

The community meetings were organized by a group called Oregon Health Decisions, which has since used focus groups in their place. Five were held in 1994, with 47 people attending and a maximum of 10 in each group. Care was taken to ensure that attendees were representative of a wider population. The structured group interview method that was employed has been found to be an effective means of eliciting public values as well as of securing reactions to such issues as the use of practice guidelines and restrictions on medical technology.[2]

In Oregon as well as elsewhere, focus groups are now considered the most effective way of extracting values from the public. However, because few people are involved, other methods are needed to secure widespread acceptance of rationing decisions, particularly when hard choices have to be made.

Clinical guidelines

Further modifications may be made as a result of an act passed by the Oregon legislature in 1993. This calls for clinical guidelines to be set for line items with the possible result that treatment could be provided to, or withheld from, some patients without regard to list placement. Thus, treatment for a condition that is funded might be withheld if the patient involved was not likely to benefit from it, and the opposite might apply to treatment for a condition which is not funded.

To make the list manageable and to reduce the number of line items involved, placements were based on the averages of patient age, duration of benefit and cost (and on quality of well-being scores before these had to be removed). This resulted in chronic rhinitis not being funded despite the fact that providers indicated that treatment is beneficial in some people with severe chronic rhinitis. A guideline is being developed to cover such instances.

However, the process of preparing guidelines is both time-consuming and complex. The whole list will not be covered. Preparation will be limited to items of clinical significance in terms of frequency of provision, high cost and high practice variation. The maximum number is being restricted to eight every two years, but at the moment the pace has been set at only two per year. There are 744 line items on the current list and, even if only one-fifth or about 150 are judged to be clinically significant, the process will take 75 years to complete.

Data deficiencies

Very few outcome data were available to prepare the Oregon list. Literature reviews were conducted, but with so many conditions to cover they were not thoroughly carried out. A large element of subjective judgement went into the process and the priority rankings need to be carefully reviewed. It has been suggested that a similar rank order would have been produced even without the complex methodology employed.

The federal Agency for Health Care Policy and Research (AHCPR) in Washington is doing a more thorough job of outcome assessment as part of its task of preparing clinical guidelines. But it is a slow and time-consuming procedure. Eventually, some items on the Oregon list may be reranked on the basis of AHCPR data.

DALYs in place of QALYs

Removal of quality of life considerations from the 1992 list in Oregon may force the AHCPR to change the way it prepares clinical guidelines. It is conducting a project under which quality of well-being scores are based on the average of those assigned by persons who are disabled and those who are not. Oregon apparently relied largely on the latter, which was the main objection to its method.

In place of QALYs, disability-adjusted life years (DALYs) will be used. With QALYs, no value is given for the extra years of life at lower quality; DALYs take account of full life expectancy regardless of quality. Although those involved in the preparation of the Oregon list prefer the methods used to rank the rejected 1991 list, they accept the need to make this change in methodology.

Effect on outcome may still be considered

It is important to note that the federal rejection of quality of life considerations was not intended to stop clinician judgement of outcome. The separate listing and low ranking assigned to liver transplants for alcoholics had to be removed because alcoholics are considered to be disabled persons, but provision could still be denied if a poor outcome was expected.

Similarly, the separate listing and low ranking assigned to life support for extremely low-birthweight babies had to be removed because it was seen as a potential violation of child protection laws, but treatment such as surfactant drugs may still be withheld if the parents agree. The federal government was concerned only when such exclusions were explicitly stated on the priority list.

Similar qualifications apply to age and lifestyle factors generally. They were ruled out as considerations in setting priorities, but not if they affected outcome. Elderly persons or smokers will have the same right to heart operations as anyone else, but not if a poor outcome is expected. This no doubt will be made clearer in the guidelines now under preparation.

However, until the Oregon plan fully incorporates and integrates individualized outcome-related decision making into its methodology and/or reimbursement schemes, this subject has little relevance to the plan. An elderly patient or smoker who is a poor surgical candidate will still have his or her operation paid for if he or she can find a willing surgeon (who participates in the plan), regardless of likely outcome, as long as the condition is ranked above the cut-off line.

Universal value of the Oregon list

However inadequate Oregon methods were, the list at least provides a template against which services can be assessed. No other priority list is available for this purpose.

Monitoring problems

Several evaluative and outcome studies of the Oregon plan are under way but the task is complicated by the fact that in Oregon, as in the USA generally, health care is provided mainly by doctors and hospitals in the private sector. This limits the state's ability to monitor services and the situation is complicated further when managed care is involved, such as that provided by health maintenance organizations (HMOs). By combining group practice with a gatekeeper role and other cost-control devices, HMOs screen access to expensive services and, as they are paid on a per capita basis, they have no incentive to maximize treatment, as is the case when fees are paid for each service.

Oregon is relying greatly on managed care to control costs; 80% of formerly eligible people and 55% of new enrollees are covered by such arrangements. But this may make it difficult to determine whether the list is being followed. The list is used to calculate the capitation rate, but detailed data must be collected to ensure compliance. The state plans to track all services through encounter data whether they fall above or below the funding line, but it remains to be seen whether large managed care organizations such as Kaiser Permanente will provide the necessary information.

References

1 Oregon Health Services Commission (1991) *Prioritization of Health Services.* A Report to the Governor and Legislature. Portland, Appendix E, p. E-1.

2 Oregon Health Decisions (1994) *Common Purpose in Health Policy – Report of Focus Group Meetings.* Oregon Health Decisions, Portland.

New Zealand

Priority setting in New Zealand relies mainly on the development of practice guidelines. No services are excluded as such from the broad range that was publicly funded when priority setting work began in 1992, but they may be withheld if not deemed appropriate to the patient involved. This, it is hoped, will eventually lead to a basic care package that is more closely defined and fairer than one in which services are excluded outright. However, guidelines will not be developed for all services, so other methods will be needed to complete the task.

Exclusions ruled out

When the Core Services Committee (CSC) was created in 1992, it was expected to proceed by way of excluding services, but this was found to be neither practical nor fair. Comprehensive services had long been provided through a state system with the exclusion of only a few services, such as adult dental care, and the public was reluctant to accept restrictions.

There was also less need to define a core, an essential precursor to the planned introduction of managed competition in 1993. Originally, it was intended to have competition on the purchasing as well as the providing side, with private insurers competing with four state regional health authorities (RHAs). Had that materialized, the definition of a core package would have been essential to ensure similar coverage, but the difficulty of setting risk-related premiums has delayed its introduction. Only the RHAs now purchase public services.

In addition, there was a conceptual reason for ruling out Oregon methods: blanket exclusions would mean that services would be denied to patients who could benefit from them. To keep the Oregon list manageable, rankings were based on averages, which took no account of cases in which treatment might prove sufficiently beneficial to warrant funding. Even the removal of tattoos might be justified if it would enable an unemployed person to find work. The saving in social costs would more than cover the expenditure involved, even without taking account of the contribution to mental health. Oregon itself has come to recognize this: through the development of clinical guidelines for each line item, it is progressively moving to allow consideration of benefit, and some flexibility is available when the degree of benefit justifies funding for excluded services in exceptional cases.

The CSC therefore took a cautious approach to defining the core. It started with the premise that existing services were suitable, representing the values of past generations of New Zealanders, but that changes might be made in the way resources were allocated. It recognized that some services had long been provided without sufficient evidence to back them, but it would take time to identify the instances in which they should be withheld. Some treatments for back pain, for example, are known to be ineffective, and guidelines are being prepared to identify those which will be excluded from the core.

Stocktake of existing services

The CSC saw its first task as taking stock of existing services and seeing if any gaps prevailed. It found inequities in the provision of primary as well as secondary care and stressed the need for a fairer allocation of resources for services such as hip replacements and heart operations. In one area, 50% of patients had to pay privately for lens replacement of cataracts, whereas in adjoining areas only 30% did. The CSC called for a critical analysis of utilization rates to provide more equal public provision.

The CSC is an advisory body, and action depends on the decisions taken by the Minister of Health, on advice from the Ministry and RHAs. RHA action has been slow in evening out disparities, and better management of waiting times is seen as a way of inducing action. In its second report, the CSC called for the abolition of waiting lists for non-urgent procedures, replacing them with a booking system under which patients would be given definite dates for specialist services.

In its report for 1995/96, the CSC goes further and suggests a system of maximum waiting times for surgery, with particular operations specified: cataract surgery, coronary artery bypass and angioplasty, hip and knee replacement, and prostate surgery. Priority is decided by a scoring system that assigns weights mainly to clinical need and likely benefit but, unlike Oregon, with some allowance for social or quality of life factors. This system is being adopted progressively by RHAs and the Minister of Health has required full implementation by 1998.

More efficient operation

In its first annual report, the CSC gave attention to the more efficient provision of existing services. For the 20 most common conditions, data were collected showing not only unit cost but the volume of services provided.

The largest total cost was attributable to normal childbirth, and the CSC suggested how savings could be realized. Bed stays in New Zealand were twice the American average; reducing them by only one day would save enough money to build a 120-bed hospital. This advice, unlike some, was acted upon: from 1 July 1996, mothers will receive a NZ$200 voucher from their RHA towards the cost of home help, domestic support and nappy laundering services if they leave hospital within 48 hours of a normal birth. Bed stays are expected to shorten as a result.

Similar data have since been extended to cover 467 conditions based on the American-inspired DRG (diagnostic-related group) classification. A three-year period is covered, with average length of stay figures shown along with cost and volume. This may enable efficiency-promoting measures similar to the one on normal childbirth to be implemented, but the same data have yet to be collected for disability support services. Such data are urgently needed since all these services have recently been put under RHA control.

In its first annual report for 1993/94, in addition to childbirth, the following diagnoses among the 20 most common conditions were singled out for attention: asthma, gastroenteritis and digestive disorders, back problems not involving surgery, stroke, ear infections and related disorders among children, chronic obstructive lung disease, heart failure and shock, and hip and knee joint replacement. Now that more comprehensive data are available, it may be possible to shorten bed stays or adopt other efficiency-promoting measures across a broad front.

Location of high-technology services

The land mass of New Zealand is the same size as that of the UK, yet it has a population of only 3.4 million compared with the UK's 57.6 million. This makes it necessary to concentrate some high-technology services at national or regional level. It is also needed to ensure a sufficient number of patients for competent provision.

The services first affected were kidney and liver transplants, along with neonatal care of tiny babies. In its latest report, the CSC calls for the extension of the same principle to a wide array of services for cancer, general surgery, gynaecology, orthopaedics and rheumatology.

Integrated planning

More efficient operation could also be secured through integrated planning and purchasing. Too many services are duplicated – as, for example, when hospitals repeat investigations already carried out by GPs. Nor is co-ordination achieved when hospitals fail to notify GPs when patients have been discharged.

More than physical health may have to be considered, particularly where disabled patients are concerned. Heavy wheelchairs may be suitable for home use but not elsewhere.

The CSC called on RHAs to adopt a holistic approach to purchasing so that services were provided in a comprehensive, integrated and co-ordinated manner. Whether this will be achieved remains to be seen.

Priority areas for health gain

As part of its task to devise a satisfactory method for setting priorities, the CSC consulted widely with the public. Based on preferences expressed by committees during consultations, the committee called for health gain priorities to be set in six areas, the first three taking precedence.

First-order priorities:

- mental health and substance abuse
- children's health services
- integrated community care services, including appropriate and culturally acceptable services for Maori.

Second-order priorities:

- emergency ambulance services
- hospice services
- habilitation/rehabilitation services.

To what extent have these priorities been implemented?

Mental health

With regard to mental health, it is impossible to answer this question without more detailed information, which is being collected. RHAs have been instructed to develop specific levels of services, but thus far the focus has been on the few who experience serious mental disorder rather than on the many who present with mental health problems at the level of primary care. The CSC has called for more attention to the latter as well as the development of strategies to provide early intervention in the community. However, it recognizes that the greater share of resources should go to those with serious disorders.

Children's health

With regard to children's health, more specific instructions have been given and RHAs have taken some action, particularly in raising the rate of child immunization from a low level. Additional services have also been purchased for the treatment of children with glue ear in order to reduce waiting times. However, it is too early to evaluate the impact of planning changes.

Maori health

In its stocktake of existing services, the CSC found hospital discharge rates for Maoris to be higher than for non-Maoris. It suggested that this might be due not only to a higher burden of illness but to less effective primary care services, thereby producing a need for hospital admission.

The CSC called for the development of effective primary care services and provided in a form that was culturally appropriate. Maoris make use of traditional healers and see health in a wider context than personal care. This made it essential to involve them in shaping priorities, as well as to increase the number of Maori providers delivering services to Maori, which has influenced the purchasing decisions of RHAs. A number of services has been developed with the emphasis on community and primary care, but the effects on Maori health and hospital discharge rates are not yet known.

Defining the core

The main task before the CSC was to determine some way of defining core services and allocating resources among them. If satisfactory priorities were to be set, then some services would be better funded than others.

At the outset, a list on the Oregon model had been ruled out. Instead, existing services were accepted as an 'implicit core', but this was seen as 'a transition measure, to minimize disruption to current effective services'. It was acknowledged that ineffective services were included but that this would take time to sort out. A more rational and explicit basis had to be devised.

Guidelines, not exclusions

Initially, some exclusions were contemplated. It was thought the core might be defined by means of a limited negative list, but this meant that whole treatments would be excluded even when they might be warranted in specific instances. Thus, the CSC decided that the key consideration would be the benefit of 'a particular service to a particular person at a particular time'. The method by which that could be most appropriately determined was the preparation of practice guidelines.

In its initial work, the CSC began to develop such guidelines. Although wider priority setting methods had to be devised, guidelines for specific conditions could be set by means of consensus conferences and 18 have since been prepared.

They are called *boundary* guidelines so as to stress the fact that they are intended for guidance only and leave scope for clinical judgement. They can be audited only across a population of patients, not on a case-by-case basis. The latter is dealt with by *protocols*, which are much more rigid, setting forth step-by-step rules of procedure that should be rigorously followed. For example, they would be used to check anaesthesia machines or for cardiopulmonary resuscitation.

The topics chosen had to be ones that were subject to widespread concern but which were likely to produce a consensus of general application. Over 120 professionals and lay experts were involved in the consensus conferences, covering such services as hip replacements, treatment of end-stage kidney failure, heart operations, life support for premature babies of extremely low birthweight (under 1000 grams) and well-child care. The first guidelines issued were criticized for not containing enough detail; this defect has since been remedied.

Age limits for renal dialysis and transplants

The age of the patient was not explicitly stated in the guidelines for heart operations, but it did occupy a prominent place in the treatment of kidney failure. Based on current clinical practice, the guideline noted that patients over 75 are usually not considered for dialysis or transplants, whereas children under five would not normally be accepted unless there was prospect of a transplant from a live donor.

Life support for low-birthweight babies was not given a cut-off point as it was at one stage in Oregon (500 grams being set). However, the disability burden that might be imposed on parents was to be discussed with them and their wishes were to be considered. If the parents agreed, life support might be withheld.

Guidelines on prescribing medicines

Five guidelines were prepared for disability support services and four affected primary care. All of the latter concerned the prescribing of medicines – minor tranquillizers, management of hypertension, hormone replacement therapy and management of dyspepsia.

The guideline on hypertension appears to have made an impact, with prescribing costs being reduced as the result of a shift from the use of expensive ACE inhibitors to low-dose diuretics and beta blockers. However, the effect of the other guidelines is not certain, and the CSC thinks GP use might be stimulated in various ways. In the first instance, it might be done through greater partnerships with professional groups in developing and promulgating such guidelines. At the other extreme, financial incentives could be employed or explicit contracts might be used with some form of audit.

Because of decades of private practice and funding mechanisms, especially fee-for-service, primary care occupies an independent place, but the other guidelines fall under RHA control. Some form of audit or data collection will be needed to determine whether they are being implemented.

Even if doctors do follow them, the guidelines may not cut costs. They were usually prepared with only effectiveness in mind, not efficiency. Most make recommendations that would require additional funding.

Other methods needed

It was recognized that guidelines could not be set for the whole of health care. Not only are they time-consuming and costly to prepare, but sufficient evidence does not always exist to secure a consensus. Therefore, work was concentrated on high-cost, high-volume procedures of wide public concern. It would cover terms of access as well as quality standards and set a model for the rest of the sector.

The details could be developed not only by guidelines but through service specifications set by RHAs or projects started by professional bodies. New technologies were to be carefully evaluated, and those at an early stage of development would not be added to the core.

This method was in essence a 'bite-size chunk' approach to priority setting, using the results as a guide to the rest of the sector. It provided a means of setting priorities within service areas but not between them. Some other means had to be devised to determine how resources should be allocated across the whole of health care.

Four criteria

The CSC recognized that no precise method could be devised; judgements would have to be made, and to facilitate those only a philosophical framework could be prepared. After extensive public consultation, four criteria were set, posed in the form of questions:

1. What are the benefits of a service?
2. Is it value for money?
3. Is it fair?
4. Is it consistent with communities' values?

In answering the first two, data might be available with regard to outcome and cost-effectiveness which could facilitate consideration. However, the last two involve judgemental assessments of equity and morality, and they would be more difficult to determine.

The most important and complex criterion is the one on fairness. By comparing relative benefits, a way might be found of shifting resources across specialties, but it was proposed that this be done through small changes so as not to shock the system.

Implementation problems

In its initial work, the CSC only indicated in broad terms the health gain areas to which resources should be directed and, although no detailed data were available, it was thought that RHAs had made some start in this way. But no volume targets had been set and, although 'service obligations' were specified by the Ministry of Health, the RHAs were free to apply them based on their own consultations with their communities over priorities.

Core service obligations of RHAs are described in nine broad categories as follows:

1. primary care (general)
2. pregnancy and childbirth
3. dental
4. primary diagnostic and therapeutic support
5. secondary (routine specialist care) and tertiary (highly specialized care) medical
6. secondary and tertiary surgical
7. mental health
8. disability support
9. specified requirements for cervical screening.

Unlike the categories used in Oregon, these were not set in priority order. They were proposed as a means to classifying services so that access and quality targets could be set for each, not to determine which should be ranked above the other. This would give the public a clearer idea of the services they could expect.

For example, with regard to dental services, schoolchildren were to receive a full range of preventive, educative and restorative services, based on at least one examination per year. Any treatment needed was to be provided within two months of the annual examination date. Also, where the clinics were not sited on school grounds, the services had to be accessed by 90% of the population within 30 minutes' travel by car. This added target was needed in a country with a large land mass and a small population.

It would take time to work out targets in this way and a start is being made with key core services. For the rest, RHAs are to make contracts with providers based on the four general criteria cited above.

How to balance resources between services

Reliance on those same four general criteria is also needed to balance resources across services. But more detailed methods are being developed, based on the data arising from access to certain elective surgical procedures.

How this will proceed is not clear, but it suggests a form of marginal analysis or programme budgeting. If sufficient cost and benefit data become available, then small changes in the present distribution of resources can be assessed and made. As an exercise in Southampton has demonstrated (see section on UK below), this does not necessarily require detailed cost–benefit studies, but judgement and intuition still play a large part in the process. There is no easy or quick fix to the task of setting priorities.

Limits on CSC influence

Thus far, CSC recommendations appear to have had only a limited influence. Where services are backed by offer to legislation, as is the case with mental health, implementation may be easier. It could also be achieved through mandated contractual arrangements, with the Ministry of Health requiring RHAs, and through them providers, to meet appropriate performance measures and confirm the targets by audit. The development of specific standards for key core services will make possible a move in that direction.

However, at present, reliance is being placed on information, persuasion and partnerships with professionals to achieve policy implementation. Only if this fails will mandates be applied.

In two notable instances, progress to implementation revealed the need for the CSC to make clearer 'the next steps' following its advice. The first involved treatment of peptic ulcer. This can be performed with better outcomes and at much lower cost through eradication of *Helicobacter pylori*, but endoscopies are required and, despite pleas from GPs and specialists, RHAs have failed to purchase sufficient of them to allow full implementation of this advice.

The other instance involved denial of renal dialysis to a 76-year-old patient with heart disease and a history of cancer. This was in line with the guideline for this service, which suggested that people over age 75 should not normally receive dialysis. The renal physician involved had helped prepare the guideline but he encouraged the patient to make a public protest. This produced such an outcry that the hospital responsible reversed the earlier decision and approved dialysis. Subsequently, the RHA that purchased the service increased funding for dialysis across the region despite the fact that it already had spent much more proportionately (in relation to population) than other parts of the country.

In 1995, the CSC's role was extended to include the independent advice functions formerly covered by the Public Health Commission. This will enable it to put more effort into preventive services, but it may have to tread warily. The Public Health Commission was abolished because some of its advice was politically uncomfortable and possibly unrealistic. For example, it called for a decrease in the consumption of dairy products on which the economy depended.

The CSC role may also be influenced by the coming general election. Henceforth, elections will be based on the principle of proportional representation, which is likely to produce a coalition government reluctant to restrict services. If that happens, the CSC could be abolished or its functions limited, with its name changed to move away from the notion of 'core' or restricted services.

Despite recognition of the value of much of its work, the CSC is suffering from a widespread perception that it has failed to address the main issue. In place of the simple list approach followed in Oregon, it has pursued a variety of methods with, thus far, little to show for it. According to one expert observer: 'Services are largely as before and change, if anything, is more difficult.'[1]

Reference

1 Cooper M H (1995) Core services and the New Zealand Health reform. *British Medical Bulletin* **51**: 799–807.

The Netherlands

Initially, priority setting was to proceed by way of exclusions, with a list inspired by the Oregon model, but now the focus is on clinical guidelines. The intention was to develop a restricted basic package of care with priorities favouring the chronic sick and vulnerable groups, such as the mentally ill, but neither the public nor politicians were ready to accept it. Although a few services have been excluded, the focus has shifted from the national to the local level, with practice guidelines as the main instrument for making choices for appropriate care.

Funnel with four sieves

Priority setting began in the wake of proposals to reform an insurance-based system of health care. Instead of 60% of the population being covered by mandatory sickness funds, everyone would be enrolled, with competition on the purchasing as well as the providing side. This has yet to be realized and action has been postponed until 1996 at the earliest.

In 1990, the Dunning Committee was appointed to advise on how priorities should be set; however, before it could report, the government decided to include 95% of existing services in the basic care package. The Committee did not agree with this policy as access to facilities would be nearly unlimited. Although angered by this policy decision, the Committee developed the so-called Dutch funnel for setting priorities, designed to screen out services through four sieves (Figure 2):

1. Is the care necessary from the community point of view?
2. Has it been demonstrated to be effective?
3. Is it efficient, using such methods as technology assessment?
4. Can it be left to individual responsibility, so that patients would pay for care themselves?

Individuals and doctors might take a different view of necessary care, but the Committee felt that the community approach should predominate. By this, it meant that health would be defined as the potential for every member of society to function normally. That enabled the Committee to give priority to the chronic sick and vulnerable groups such as the elderly and mentally ill.

The second sieve requires evidence of effective care and the third sieve selects on efficiency. Applied strictly, these two sieves would exclude a large proportion of care from the basic package. The fourth sieve excludes care that can be left to individual responsibility, having patients to pay for it themselves.

However, the final package of necessary care would be determined not by costs per QALY or an assessment of public preferences, but by political considerations. Dunning presented an instrument for priority setting and strongly

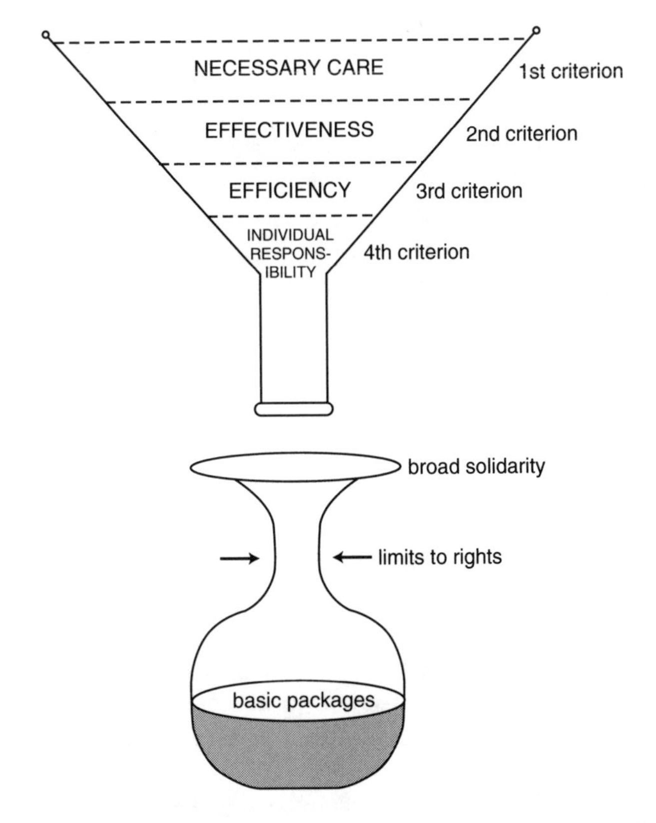

Figure 2: The Dunning Committee's four 'sieves' for health services.

recommended the Cabinet to apply the method in order to have a restricted basic package.

Reaction of the Ministry of Health

At first the funnel idea received a hostile reaction, particularly from the civil servants at the Ministry of Health.

Gradually, the process of deinsuring was accepted. Homeopathic medicines were the first to be removed from the package and dental care for adults is being left to individual responsibility. This was in line with the funnel framework of the Dunning Committee.

Other services now the subject of an intense public debate are contraceptives, homes for the elderly and some physiotherapy. It is likely that fertility procedures, e.g. *in vitro* fertilization (IVF), and many non-essential drugs will be removed from the package, and the same applies to psychotherapy.

Waiting lists

The Dunning Committee opposed any form of rationing within the basic package. Any procedure that made its way through the four sieves could not be withheld. Only if financial resources proved insufficient might changes be made; in that case, services of low priority could be removed from the package if waiting lists for the services with higher priority became too long.

In such circumstances, waiting lists themselves would be set in priority order. At the top would come those patients who could not take care of themselves, for example demented persons and the mentally retarded. They would have priority over those waiting for heart surgery no matter how serious their condition might be.

The government accepted the analysis on waiting lists and carried out research on the problem. This showed wide variations, with some hospitals having long waits owing mainly to inefficient operation. As a consequence, a waiting list problem will not be solved primarily by injections of money.

Assessment of new technology

Dunning also proposed controls over the introduction of new technology. In the past, explicit restrictions applied only to drugs and some expensive facilities. To prevent the excessive duplication that exists in the US, hospitals need special permits before they can carry out functions such as dialysis, kidney transplantation, heart surgery and neonatal intensive care. Dunning now suggested that controls be extended so as to favour the development of new technology for the chronic sick.

The Committee felt that controls should preferably be applied within the framework of the European Community. However, since 1987 The Netherlands has established its own Fund for Investigational Medicine (MTA) to provide information about the benefits and costs of new technologies. Dunning wanted existing care added to its remit and the government agreed. A list of 126 existing technologies are being investigated in a top-down research programme through quick and dirty studies using meta-analysis. Any found to be ineffective or inefficient will be removed from the basic package through practice guidelines, protocols and consensus documents.

Guidelines for appropriate care

Dunning felt that it was not sufficient to set priorities at the national level: clinicians, insurers and patients had to make choices at the level where care is actually delivered. There, the wheat could be separated from the chaff, supplying only appropriate care that had sufficient evidence to demonstrate its cost-effectiveness.

For that purpose, clinicians would take the lead in developing guidelines but with some involvement by consumers and insurers, both of which are now to be given a more influential role; before guidelines such as those on very expensive drugs, e.g. growth hormone, are prepared, a consensus will have to be secured from all three parties.

As in Oregon, age and lifestyle *per se* have been ruled out as considerations in setting priorities.

Shift in government policy

Politicians have found it difficult to set priorities at the national level and find it easier to shift responsibility for the rising costs of health care to providers at the local level. This has produced a change in the way in which the funnel is applied; it is now promoted as a symbol for doctors to use in daily practice.

The government has a new Minister of Health with a new mission – the development of evidence-based medicine. Hopes are now pinned on the implementation of practice guidelines; they, rather than exclusions set at the national level, will mainly determine what is offered to patients.

The new Minister of Health has a long-standing interest in evidence-based medicine, having emphasized the subject while a professor of medicine at the University of Amsterdam.[1] She believes it can remove 15% of the waste that, in her view, exists in the health care system.[2] Whether this will be more effective in reducing the health care budget remains to be seen.

If it does not, then she may support the further exclusion of services on the Dunning model. In parliament, she indicated that core services could be limited to 75% of the existing package. This compares with the 95% level applied until recently and the 85% figure set by another government committee (the Dekker Committee) in 1987.

Altering public attitudes

A poll commissioned by the Dunning Committee found that the majority of the public were opposed to any restrictions on treatment, even the most expensive ones. Dunning recognized that it would take time to accustom the public to the need for making choices and proposed a three-year programme aimed at persuading influential consumer groups.

The programme started with the publication of the Dunning Report, but it was run more or less independently from the government.

The programme aimed at the public followed a bottom-up procedure, with focus groups used at the start and a large meeting at the end. It was recently completed and the effects are being evaluated. Will the public now accept restrictions on services? The government must have doubts since it has placed its stress on guideline development at the local level rather than service exclusions set nationally.

How, also, will the public react to the priorities contained in the Dunning Report? In contrast to the Oregon methods, these were set without public consultation and came down strongly in favour of the chronic sick and vulnerable groups. The three-year programme recently completed was designed not to find out what the public wanted, but to secure its assent to the priorities favoured by experts.

Will it be possible to give priority on waiting lists to persons with learning disabilities or will the public insist on treatment being given first to those needing heart operations? A survey made in 1989 about what to include in the basic package found little support for the care of persons with learning disabilities. The public considered it even less important than dental services. This contrasts with the view of the new Minister of Health, who told parliament that it was 'not acceptable to have demented elderly people or mentally handicapped children on waiting lists for care'.[2]

How this difference is resolved remains to be seen.

References

1 Sheldon T (1995) Keep taking the pill. *Health Service Journal*, 16 November, 11–15.
2 Spanjer M (1995) Changes in Dutch health-care. *Lancet* **345**: 50–51.

Norway

Health care here is under local authority control, but priority setting has developed under national direction. A framework has been established with five categories of priority for treatment: emergencies, serious cases, cases in need of treatment but not so serious, cases requiring effective treatment but whose need is not pressing and, lastly, care that is demanded but which is neither needed nor of proven value. Only the last would not be provided; it has 'zero priority'. No list has been made of specific exclusions, nor has much interest been shown in the development of clinical guidelines except for bone marrow transplantation.

Effort, rather, has been concentrated on reducing waiting lists. In Norway, a deep cultural aversion to treatment delays exists; they are considered the greatest disgrace of a health system. A six-month guarantee of treatment has been set for the serious conditions covered by category 2, but this has not resulted in a reduction in waiting lists, nor has the guarantee been completely fulfilled. Faced with a rising demand for hospital care, doctors have inflated waiting lists by adding all from category 2 who need elective treatment.

Five levels of priority care

The first attempt to set priorities was made in 1987 with the report of the government-appointed Lonning Commission. It proposed five levels of priority care, and this model was officially adopted in 1989 as part of the National Health Plan. But for several years nothing happened; no attempt was made to implement the priorities. They seem to have been intended to provide only a guide to allocating resources at the planning level, not as a way of making clinical decisions in individual cases. Rising health costs had to be restrained, but with a buoyant economy supported by abundant oil revenues Norway did not feel the same pressure as other countries.

Action on waiting lists

Efforts, rather, were concentrated on reducing long waiting lists. Extra funds were devoted to the task from 1984 but, although this enabled more patients to be treated, waiting lists were not cut.

The government thus saw fit to provide a national guarantee of treatment: all in category 2 would have to wait no more than six months. (Those in category 1 – the emergency cases – are treated within 24 hours.) Criteria were developed for every speciality based on diagnosis and the severity of symptoms; they were issued as guidelines in a broad sense by the Ministry of Health. When the guarantee was under consideration, it was expected that only three or four diagnoses would be selected, but the Lonning model was used instead.

Only limited effects

The guarantee has not been completely fulfilled, nor has it significantly reduced waiting lists. As many as 60% of the patients waiting for elective treatment fall in category 2 and the six-month limit has been met for 95% of them. But 5% still have to wait longer. Yet, most of those without a guarantee (categories 3 and 4) wait no longer than six months; not more than 20% of these patients exceed the limit.

This paradox is explained by the disparities that exist in hospital efficiency: some hospitals manage to treat more patients at a faster rate than others.

Gradually, however, waiting lists are being reduced everywhere, resulting in more nearly equal provision. This is said to be due to better co-ordination between hospitals and the application of more precise criteria by doctors. Instead of relying on diagnoses to establish the need for treatment, clinicians are attaching greater weight to the severity of symptoms.

This means that some patients are left without a guarantee and may have to wait longer than six months, but there is a general disinclination to go elsewhere for treatment. Even if a neighbouring county can offer more immediate care, more patients prefer to wait for treatment at their local hospital.

A central electronic register has been established to record waiting list figures and promote uniformity. All hospitals are required to submit data quarterly, and reports are published showing where disparities exist.

Too much attention on waiting lists

The main weakness of the system is that it focuses too much attention on waiting lists; other aspects of health care are neglected. In particular, not enough consideration is given to prevention or care for the chronic sick and vulnerable groups.

Waiting lists have a built-in bias for the acute sector: they are concerned mainly with those who need elective surgery or other forms of specialist treatment, not the community care so vital to vulnerable groups such as the mentally ill.

Debate on White Paper

These and other issues are discussed in a White Paper on Health Policy. The government favours continuation of the Lonning model for setting priorities and upholds the six-month waiting time guarantee, but it suggests adjustments in the way the system operates. These include the following:

- More attention should be paid to the harm that might be done if treatment were denied or delayed; mental and social as well as physical effects should be assessed.
- In considering priorities between treatments, the cost is to be considered only when the benefits are equal. (Oregon follows the same procedure.)
- More money should be spent on chronic disease. Specific reference is made to chronic conditions in the fields of cancer, psychiatry and orthopaedics.
- Doctors should be urged to develop clinical guidelines to promote the use of appropriate procedures and avoid those of little or no proven benefit.

- The public has not been involved in the priority setting process and measures are needed to make it more open.

More funds for health care

The waiting time guarantee is to be formally recognized in a new Law of Patient's Rights, but the main concern of the Norwegian legislature is on the funding of health care. In contrast to other countries, the government wants to spend more and the amounts involved will determine the extent to which priorities have to be set. Norway thus seems to be in the enviable position of being partly relieved of financial pressure where treatment choices have to be made.

In June 1995, parliament decided to reduce the time limit for category 2 patients to three months and to set a limit of six months for those in categories 3 and 4. But the new limits, which will not become effective until 1997, have set off a public debate. Will this induce doctors to inflate waiting lists? Are there enough doctors and nurses to fulfil the guarantee? Can it be applied in some way to cover patients with chronic and mental illnesses? Experience has shown that a guarantee of treatment given by politicians is not easily adopted at clinical level.

Sweden

Priority setting is developing slowly but is set to proceed by way of exclusions and smaller resource allocations to services of lower priority. Although a distinction is made between priorities set at the administrative and clinical levels, little attention has been given to the preparation of clinical guidelines.

Politicians are involved in the process of setting priorities. Health care is under local authority control and elected councillors determine how priorities are decided and money is spent. But they have received guidance from politicians at the national level who have set forth the ethical principles and general methods by which priorities should be determined.

Waiting list initiative

Priority setting here began with efforts to reduce long waiting lists. As in Norway, delay in securing needed treatment is seen as the greatest failing of health care. One local authority (at the Falu General Hospital) attacked the problem as early as 1987, but national action did not come until 1992. Then, all county councils were required to guarantee care for 10 diagnoses, with waits limited to no more than three months. This led to a large reduction in waiting time as a result of efficiency improvements, but it also meant that a high priority was assigned to the 10 surgical operations selected.

Stockholm adopted a technique from the US to accomplish it, reimbursing hospitals on the basis of diagnostic-related groups (DRGs). However, payments were made on a flat-rate basis instead of the variable allowance used in the US which not only produced excessive costs but failed to take account of the complexity of care.

Wider move toward priority setting

Since then, a wider move toward priority setting has begun, stimulated by financial pressures and the creation by some county councils of an internal market with a split between purchasers and providers. With health care under local authority control, methods vary greatly, but a more uniform procedure may develop as the result of action taken by the central government. It appointed a Priorities Commission to provide guidance and the commission proposed an ethical framework by which priorities should be decided.

Three principles are set forth:

1 **Human dignity.** This implies that all individuals are of equal value and that none should receive preference because of personal characteristics or status in the community. Elsewhere, this is usually considered under a principle called 'equity'.

Treatment can be withheld because it might not be of sufficient benefit, but it cannot be denied solely because of a patient's advanced age, lifestyle or, in the case of premature babies, low birthweight. Any minimum birthweight figure – such as the 500 grams once proposed in Oregon – is ruled out. However, no methods are proposed to ensure that treatment is withheld only on the basis of an assessment of outcome.

Contrary to this principle, it should be noted that those over 65 are specifically excluded from an Act designed to favour the provision of technical and other aids to those with severe functional impairments. Age was also a factor in two polls involving doctors, nurses, administrators and politicians. In one, a large majority felt that a 20-year-old should have priority over an 80-year-old in the same situation.

2 **Need and solidarity.** This qualifies the first principle since resources are not infinite. Resources must go to those who need them most, particularly vulnerable groups such as the mentally ill. Their needs cannot always be expressed and solidarity means that they should receive special consideration.

3 **Cost-efficiency.** All other considerations being equal, the most cost-efficient care should be provided. Otherwise, a reasonable relationship must be sought between cost and effectiveness of treatment with due regard for the quality of life. Only methods for treating the same disease can be approached in this way; these set priorities in the form of 'bite-size chunks'. They cannot be applied when different diseases are involved; then, the effects of treatment cannot be fairly compared.

This rules out any attempt to use QALYs across the whole of health care, as was first tried in Oregon. Even if data were available, the effects could not be fairly assessed. In any case, QALYs as a method are not favoured in Sweden because evaluation of the quality of life is based on subjective judgements and the individual involved is best able to judge it. QALYs, it is recognized, may also have a perverse effect on the elderly: the number of years of benefit that treatment will provide figures in the calculation, and this can exceed an elderly person's life expectancy.

No guidance was offered on an upper limit of expenditure for individual treatment. It was recognized that, in some instances, the benefit would not be worth the expense, but this was left to local determination. Financial pressures might force treatment to be withheld, particularly in the smaller budgetary units created by some county councils as part of an internal market.

These principles do not hold the same priority. The first comes before the second and the second before the third. Since the cost-efficiency principle comes last, this means that care must sometimes be given even when it is more expensive or would not 'pay'.

Rejected principles

Other principles were considered but rejected. One called for resources to be spent so as to benefit the greatest number of people. The commission said that no attempt should be made to help many people with mild disorders instead of a few with severe injuries.

Nor should priority be given to patients who are most profitable to society – such as younger persons in employment rather than seniors who are retired. This, again, seemed to conflict with the feeling in the opinion surveys cited above that preferential treatment should be given to the young.

The demand for services was another principle that could not be ignored, particularly when competitive pressures were involved. But it should not take preference over need.

The autonomy principle meant that patients could refuse treatment but that they could not expect to receive services of unproven benefit.

Priority order

On the basis of these principles, priorities are set on the administrative as well as the clinical level of care. Here, a model was adopted from the one used in Norway. The commission ruled out a comprehensive list on the Oregon pattern, finding this method to be too mechanical in character with no consideration for special circumstances in individual cases. Also, as in New Zealand, the commission refused to define a basic package of care, asserting that the vast majority of health care should be jointly and equitably funded.

At the administrative level, resources are to be allocated according to the assessment of needs, not the demands of those who shout the loudest, and would apply to treatment groups as a whole rather than to individuals. The latter are subject to decisions made by clinicians, who have to adjust the treatment they provide to changing conditions.

The priorities set at both levels are similar and arranged in categories like those used in Norway. As in Oregon, everyone is entitled to a diagnosis, but treatment would be provided in the following order:

1 The highest priority is given to patients with severe acute diseases that could lead to disability or death.

This priority also includes treatment of severe chronic diseases, palliative terminal care and care of persons with reduced autonomy such as the mentally ill.

At the clinical level, the mentally ill group would take slightly lower priority, life-threatening acute disease taking preference over everything else. However, stress is placed on the need to treat as emergency cases chronic patients in severe distress.

With regard to the terminally ill, the commission saw no need to prolong the process of dying if there was no hope of improvement. This applied particularly to those in chronic vegetative states or in an advanced stage of dementia, but the decision must not be influenced by financial pressures. The commission stressed the right of a dignified end to life as a top priority in medical care.

2 Prevention measures come next, but only those of documented benefit. However, all forms of prevention might be excluded if separate central finance were available. The benefits are harder to measure than where treatment is concerned and require a wider as well as a longer perspective than local authorities can provide.

Rehabilitative services, together with the provision of technical aids to disabled persons, are also included in this priority.

3 Less severe disease comes next, with preference, as in all groups, given to persons likely to receive greater benefit from treatment. This is not intended to give preference to acute cases that are easily treated as opposed to the chronic ill, for whom the benefits of treatment are less evident. However, no guidance is offered as to how this preference might be avoided.

4 This covers care for borderline cases, such as those suffering from involuntary childlessness. If resources are limited, treatment might be restricted in various ways, or charges raised in the amount patients have to pay.

Only in extreme cases would treatment be provided for shortness of stature not due to hormonal causes. Psychotherapy would be similarly restricted to those suffering from some form of accepted mental disorder, not to persons troubled by personality or emotional problems.

5 This covers care for reasons other than disease or injury and would not be publicly funded.

Only the first three priorities would qualify for resource allocations at the administrative level. Priority 5 was covered by priority 4 in the earlier report issued for discussion purposes. As a result of the comments received, priority 4 is now confined to borderline cases for whom care might or might not be provided. Previously, priority 5 covered minor ailments for which self-care would suffice and, presumably, they are now included in priority 4 with borderline cases.

Advice on implementation

Guidance was also offered on how these principles and priorities should be implemented. Resources were to be allocated in descending order of priority, but stress was placed on the need to shift more money in favour of the second group in priority 1.

Too few funds, it is stressed, are devoted to the care of those with severe chronic diseases, the terminally ill and vulnerable groups such as the mentally ill. They do not receive a fair share in comparison with those in priorities 2 and 3. It does not seem just that those with less severe disease should receive a larger proportion of funds. If resource gaps appeared, then the commission favoured service exclusions rather than reductions in the quality of care given to those in the most vulnerable groups.

Warnings are also given against reductions in care to vulnerable groups as a result of the competitive pressures introduced by the internal market and performance-related payments. Elderly persons may be less 'profitable' to treat than younger persons, but preference should not be given to younger people for that reason.

Concern was expressed about the size of the budgetary units formed under the internal market created by some councils. Large ones are better able than small ones to absorb the cost of expensive cases, for example a case of lower priority but one that the doctors involved believe merits exceptional treatment. In such instances, doctors are free to meet the expense with the funds in their own unit, but must not neglect the needs of patients with higher priorities.

Although social services were not specifically included in the commission's remit, they are closely connected with health care, and the commission believed that the same ethical principles should apply. However, it recognized that priorities in welfare generally would have to be set by political considerations. It therefore called attention only to areas where co-operation is essential or was deficient. For example, patients with long-term mental disorders need not only medical treatment but assistance with housing, occupation and social training.

Action by local authorities

Although priority setting methods vary by locality, the main aim has been to provide services more efficiently, abolish waiting lists for critical procedures and distribute resources more fairly. In this respect, the Swedish processes resemble the programme started in New Zealand, although it is only recently that attention has been given to the development of clinical guidelines. For the most part, they are being left, as the Priorities Commission suggested, to the discretion of the senior consultants in charge of clinical specialties.

Although Swedish interest in priority setting was inspired by the Oregon example, only one county council has seen fit to prepare a detailed list. Sweden is moving ahead cautiously with scope allowed for local variation so that different methods may be tried.

Of the 23 county councils and three large municipalities, only four have been actively engaged in the process: Dalarna (Falun), Stockholm, Gavleborg and Vasterbotten. In Falun, GP fundholders were once used but have now been phased out.

Progress has been somewhat delayed by the creation of the Priorities Commission. Vasterbotten thought that the commission's report would settle the problem, not realizing that only general principles would be proposed. However, as noted below, these are likely to have some effect on the methods thus far employed.

Falu's 'waiting list' model

The oldest and most developed method started at the Falu General Hospital in 1987. It is concerned mainly with securing a fairer distribution of resources across specialties and, although outpatients are covered, primary care personnel find it geared more to inpatients. That is why it is often described as 'a waiting list model'.

Priority setting here is thus mainly limited to hospital care. Community services are largely left untouched, which will make it difficult to shift resources in favour of the chronic sick and vulnerable groups as the commission desires. Many services for the mentally ill are provided in the community – yet in the Falu model they may receive a smaller proportion of resources than goes towards reducing waiting lists for treatment of the less severe diseases included in priority level 3, which includes surgery for non-emergency conditions such as inguinal hernia and varicose veins. Both fall below the funding line in Oregon and are not provided at all.

Stockholm's 'bite-size chunk' approach

Stockholm is pursuing a 'bite-size chunk' approach, confining itself to specific conditions of illness and not attempting to set priorities across the whole of health care. The aim is to determine how to distribute resources between prevention, acute services and rehabilitation. In pursuing this course, Stockholm took the lead from an experiment conducted at Southampton in the UK by Chris Ham and Chris Heginbotham.[1]

One district chose cancer as a pilot study and the techniques employed were demonstrated at a seminar. Use of this method depends on sufficient information being available about costs, volume, outcome and the availability of other relevant data. Because of data deficiencies, not all priorities can be set in this way, and the method offers no means of deciding how to allocate resources across the whole of health care.

Furthermore, the method depends on the availability of reliable information, which may be difficult to obtain in the chronic sector. This approach is thus more suitable for acute conditions and the procedure can complicate decision-making if choices are allowed to lie on the table. That is what happened in Southampton and it accentuates the need to find a way of making choices across the whole of health care. Stockholm has used this method to base purchases on packages of care, but here also not all choices have been implemented.

Stockholm will thus have to develop new techniques to set priorities in the manner recommended by the commission, particularly if resources are to be shifted in favour of the chronic sick and vulnerable groups such as the mentally ill.

Gavleborg's category model

Gavleborg is producing a model using methods similar to those employed in Oregon, but it has not yet been implemented as it was proposed only for discussion purposes.

Before priorities are set, the council wants to make its delivery system more efficient and, with the aid of clinical guidelines, discontinue treatments that are of little or no benefit. This stage of the programme is similar to the one employed in New Zealand.

Gavleborg is also intent on securing a consensus among politicians, doctors and the public. If this is pursued, public consultation is likely to take a more active form than it has done elsewhere in Sweden.

To prepare the way, ethical principles have been prepared, among which four are stressed: equality, autonomy, the need to avoid injury to the patient and the number of patients affected. The last conflicts with those proposed by the Priorities Commission, since it was specifically rejected. The commission did not feel preference should be given to the many people with mild disorders instead of the few with severe injuries.

Age and lifestyle *per se* have been ruled out as considerations in priority setting but, as the Priorities Commission proposed, they may well be taken into account in assessing outcome. The need for well-documented results is stressed, but Gavleborg recognizes that this cannot always be achieved and that consideration may have to be given to another test – a wide consensus as to the positive effects of treatment. This is in contrast to the Dunning model in the Netherlands, in which the use of 'sieves' means that all care not rigorously shown to be effective would apparently be excluded from the basic package.

To set priorities, a preliminary classification of services has begun, putting them into four categories similar to the five priorities proposed by the Priorities Commission. The main difference lies in the way in which minor or self-limiting conditions are classified. In Gavleborg, they come in the fourth category and hold the lowest priority, but treatments for them are divided into two sections – those with documented benefit and those without. The Priorities Commission did not specifically make this distinction but probably intended all to be included in priority 4 dealing with borderline cases. It reserved priority 5 for care required for reasons other than disease and this was not to be publicly funded.

Classification has thus far been confined to conditions dealing with the main specialties, and it is not at all certain that sufficient attention will be given to the chronic sick and vulnerable groups. The various medical specialists involved are being given the opportunity to challenge each other in an attempt to secure consensus, but the final decision will be made by members of the Gavleborg Council. It remains to be seen whether they will shift resources towards the chronic sector as the Priorities Commission has recommended.

Vasterbotten's concern for vulnerable groups

Among all the councils, Vasterbotten has shown the greatest concern for vulnerable groups, giving them the same high priority (second only to those in need of life-saving treatment) as the Priorities Commission.

Vasterbotten had also progressed the furthest, intending to implement the procedure it had prepared, not just propose it for study or discussion. But that aim has been delayed: Vasterbotten expected the report of the Priorities Commission to settle the problem and put its own programme on hold. Now that only a general framework has been proposed, the council will renew action, but it should have little difficulty making its priorities conform to those set nationally.

The main issue may concern treatment for low-birth-weight babies. Priority setting began here as the result of the media attention created by one councillor who questioned the wisdom of such treatment. The Priorities Commission has since specifically ruled out minimum weight limits in such cases, but still left room for treatment to be withheld because of insufficient benefit.

The procedure to be used here has two parts: one concerned with information regarding treatment, the other with the priority to be assigned to it. The first will be provided by clinicians and include such data as the need, effects and cost of treatment. The second will be decided by the members of the council, using their own scale of ethical priorities. For the most part, the latter conform to those set by the Priorities Commission.

The procedure is designed to deal with particular treatments, but the council also wants to use it to cover the whole process of resource allocation, including the preparation of budgets and an assessment of results.

Public consultation

Little has been attempted in the way of public consultation. Politicians fear the electoral consequences, and only one council, Gavleborg, has clearly recognized the need.

It may be argued that the need is less pressing in a system under local authority control, with democratic elections and councillors purporting to represent the views of the public. But these views may be difficult to determine in an area so strewn with ethical questions as one concerned with the setting of priorities in health care.

Dr Stefan Holmström (formerly Acting Director at the Department of Community Medicine at Huddinge Hospital and Medical Advisor at the Federation of Swedish County Councils, now with Bure Health Care) has taken the lead in promoting public consultation and two surveys instigated by the Priorities Commission: one seeking views on priorities from a nationwide sample of 1500 persons between the ages of 18 and 84, the other directing similar questions at 300 doctors and 300 nurses.

The Federation of Swedish County Councils also sponsored a survey of 571 persons in four counties, composed of 168 politicians, 144 administrators and 259 physicians. It sought their views on the ethics and priorities of health care.

In Stockholm, the views of 671 doctors and nurses at five hospitals were obtained in a study conducted by the Department of Community Medicine at Huddinge Hospital. However, this was concerned with the changes made in service provision, particularly from the introduction of DRGs.

The survey of the general public gave strong support to the principles adopted by the Priorities Commission, but about half the doctors and nurses in the national survey felt that age should be a factor in setting priorities. A large majority held the same view in the study sponsored by the Federation of Swedish County Councils.

Reference

1 Ham C and Heginbotham C with Cochrane M and Richards J (1992) *Purchasing Dilemmas*. King's Fund College, London.

United Kingdom

Priority setting in the UK is proceeding mainly by the development of clinical guidelines rather than the exclusion of services. The Department of Health publishes guidance on planning and priorities each year, while regional bodies make efforts to secure compliance. Specific priorities are left to local interpretation, but the need to meet national targets such as those on waiting lists may override local preferences.

Movement for evidence-based medicine

Through its research and development programme, the Department of Health has led a movement for evidence-based medicine that is attracting worldwide attention. National support has been provided for the evaluation of new technologies, with centres established at Oxford (UK Cochrane Centre) and York (Centre for NHS Reviews and Dissemination) to collect, evaluate and distribute relevant data on the effectiveness and cost of treatment. Periodically, bulletins are issued for guidance on specific conditions and one showed how clinical guidelines might best be implemented.[1] Two Executive Letters published by the NHS Executive (a national body charged with responsibility for implementing policy) have been issued, stimulating effort at the local level to develop clinical guidelines.[2,3]

No national initiative to guide priorities

The UK is the only one of the countries studied where the government has resisted suggestions for a national initiative to debate and determine priorities. An official committee of the legislature called for explicit ethical principles to be set, such as those dealing with equity, choice and effectiveness, but no action of this kind has been forthcoming.[4] Instead, the government sees no need to ration core services when so much scope exists to eliminate ineffective procedures.[5]

Some shifts in resources have occurred, but only to a modest extent. To the degree that any general direction exists, attempts favour a switch from acute to primary and community care.[6] The Department of Health favours this movement, but local efforts are being frustrated by national targets focused on the acute sector. This applies particularly to a directive to reduce waits for elective surgery to a maximum of one year.

Background

Priority setting has existed since the NHS began, but previously took the form mainly of waiting lists for treatment. Access to only a few costly services, such as renal dialysis, were subject to age or other restrictions. Decisions were made mainly by clinicians behind closed doors. The public had no place and little influence on the process; only community health councils (statutory bodies created in each district to represent patients) might occasionally make their views felt.

Internal market reforms

The reforms introduced in 1991 made a sharp break with the past. An internal market was introduced, and this created pressure to make priority setting more explicit. With purchasers separated from providers, both began to look more critically at the services offered.

One regional health authority went so far as to suggest that patients waiting for certain services be removed from waiting lists, thus requiring them to pay for their own treatment. But the Department of Health forced it to rescind the decision. The NHS Act calls for a comprehensive service and that, ministers maintain, must be upheld.

Nevertheless, those concerned with purchasing services at a local level remained free to exclude services if they wished. This applies now not only to district health authorities and GP fundholders, who hold budgets of their own, but also to the new commissioning agencies, which will be responsible for the provision of all services, including those of family practitioners, which were previously administered by a separate authority.

Variation in local provision

Despite ministerial discouragement, some health authorities and GP fundholders have chosen to exclude services. Although only a few services have been dropped, this has produced an anomalous situation with exclusions nominally barred but allowed at local level. As a result, regional disparities have arisen that are undermining long-standing efforts to secure uniform provision. Some health authorities exclude services which neighbouring ones offer. In one notable instance involving IVF, this generated bitter resentment from women who had been denied access.

Disparities also exist as a result of clinical discretion. Some surgeons have refused to perform heart operations on smokers, while elderly patients may be denied access to renal dialysis and other expensive procedures. Here, the assessment of outcome is said to be controlling; treatment, the Department of Health maintains, is not denied because of age or lifestyle alone. But a procedure has yet to be devised to ensure that this is so.

Guiding principles sought

Some agonizing decisions have had to be made without national guidance. One involved the denial of a second bone marrow transplant to a child suffering from leukaemia. With only a slight chance of survival, the health authority argued that the benefit did not seem worth the suffering the child would have to undergo. Others, however, disagreed and the authority that made the decision was subjected to a barrage of media criticism.

Though the cost involved was said not to be a factor, there was some suspicion that it was, and the legislative committee cited above (House of Commons Select Committee on Health) called for clearer rulings on funding. Pressures are thus building in the UK for a stronger lead from the centre.

Push for evidence-based medicine

Meanwhile, national effort is concentrated on the development of evidence-based medicine. Decisions are still left to local action, but the Department of Health has urged purchasers to base them increasingly on evidence of clinical effectiveness.

In particular, a strong lead has been given to the development of clinical guidelines. The movement has only just begun and the results are uncertain. Since some guidelines could increase expenditure rather than reduce it, the impact may be greater on the quality of care than on its cost.[7]

Priority setting at the local level

Local discretion has left room for a variety of methods to be employed. Although interest has been shown in the Oregon experiment, no attempt has been made to compile a detailed list. The task is beyond the capacity of individual authorities, and many consider the method too mechanistic. Furthermore, the Department of Health has set itself firmly against it. More interest is being shown in New Zealand methods since they are similar to those used in the UK.

In the process of setting priorities, decisions are influenced by those taken at five levels, beginning with the funding allocations made by central government and the Department of Health, and ending with clinician selections of patients to treat and the amounts to be spent.[8] In the middle lies the crucial decisions to be made at district level, and there competing pressures have to be balanced. These have been usefully presented on a figure devised by Chris Ham and Chris Heginbotham in connection with a

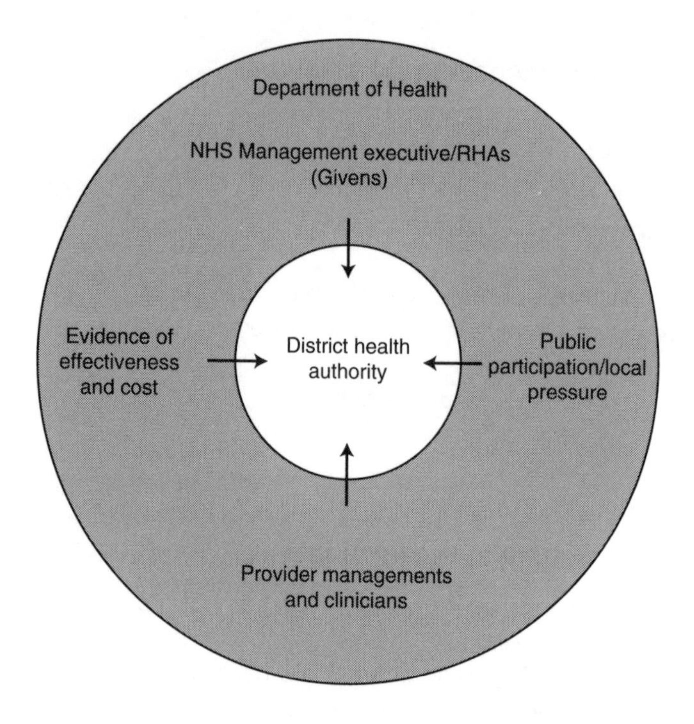

Figure 3: Sources of pressures on district health authorities. (Devised by Chris Ham and Chris Heginbotham.)

pioneering experiment in priority setting at Southampton in 1991 (Figure 3).[9]

From above come the directives and targets set by the Department of Health and regional health authorities. From below arise the demands of clinicians and providers; their co-operation must be secured before priorities can be implemented.

These pressures have always existed, but since the 1991 reforms two have been added: health authorities must increasingly take account of public opinion on the one hand and evidence of treatment on the other, considering not only its effectiveness but its cost.

How priorities are set

To show how these pressures might be resolved, periodic surveys have been made of the way in which health authorities set priorities. Some shift has occurred in the direction of community services and care for the chronic sick, but acute services in the hospital sector still receive more than their fair share of development funding. On average, each purchaser funds 15 or 16 priorities.[10]

In the first three years following the 1991 reform, only a few authorities (12 out of 114 surveyed in 1992, 4 out of 100 in 1993, 11 out of 108 in 1994) denied or limited specific forms of treatment, confining action mainly to marginal procedures such as tattoo removal.[6,10,11] In 1995, however, nearly a third (40 out of 129) did so, with exclusions extending to such procedures as insertion of grommets (23), dilatation and curettage in women aged under 40 (21) and treatment for varicose veins (10).[12]

The new Secretary of State for Health has now called for a halt to this movement, allowing only the 'sensible' use of clinical guidelines to decide when treatment should be withheld.[13] This puts the Department of Health firmly behind the movement to stimulate the development of evidence-based medicine. At the local level, clinical guidelines are thus likely to remain the preferred policy.

Detailed studies at district level

A detailed study of the way in which priorities are set in six pacesetting districts was conducted in 1992.[14] As was the case generally, few changes had been made. Restrained by calls to keep a 'steady state', health authorities produced only a modest shift in resources. On the whole, they did not exclude services, but showed a growing interest in developing clinical guidelines designed to identify patients who would benefit from treatment.

The widest scope for setting priorities was provided by growth money to finance service development. A wide range of methods were used, including questionnaires and scoring systems to rank bids presented by providers.

A step-by-step look at the process

The Southampton Health Commission has exposed its procedures to public view. It did so first in a simulation seminar conducted in 1991;[9] then, in 1995, it did so through an actual process of priority setting.[15]

In the sections which follow, the methods used in this 1995 exercise are described. Several are novel and provide an example for others to follow. However, the exercise was complicated by the number of choices which had to be considered, and some means of restricting these has to be devised.

Southampton was also fortunate in having growth money at its disposal. It thus did not have to make the hard choices facing those authorities which have to cope with cuts in spending. Southampton found it possible to rule out service exclusions and concern itself solely with how growth money should be apportioned; other authorities may not have this option.

Stocktake of existing services

The process should logically begin with a stocktake of existing services, but many districts fail to do so.[6] Those that do seldom do so to the level of detail supplied in New Zealand. Some limit information to an outline of the current configuration of services, indicating only the number of acute hospitals and the services they provide as opposed to the pattern of services in primary care. The more ambitious provide data by health programme (e.g. cancers, mental health), with volume and expenditure amounts given for individual care and client groups.

Needs assessment

The next step in the process is to make an assessment of needs, usually in the form of a broad epidemiological framework. The UK is unique in this respect; no similar efforts are made elsewhere, except at the regional level in New Zealand. However, the amount of detail supplied varies enormously, and methods are needed to establish a closer link with purchasing decisions. In particular, areas have to be identified where service provision fails to satisfy needs. Only in that way can maximum benefits be secured for the local population.

In deciding how growth money is to be spent, bids are usually invited from clinicians in provider units and a shortlist is prepared for the health authority to consider. The shortlist is often compiled by those who make the assessment of needs – a procedure carried out under the lead of a medically qualified director of public health. It is then considered by the members of the purchasing team before being referred to the health authority.

Several criteria may be employed, but the one usually felt to be most important is concerned with what is called 'health gain', or the extent to which the proposal will contribute to the overall health of the local population. However, allocation decisions can also be strongly influenced by considerations of equity, or the extent to which the needs of individuals or special groups (such as ethnic minorities or rural populations) are satisfied. The provision of accessible and equitable services was found to be the dominant value guiding health authorities in a survey of 66 strategy plans in 1994.[6]

Two-stage scoring process

At one of the six pacesetting authorities studied in 1992 (then called City and Hackney, now East London and City), a formal two-stage scoring system was used to set priorities for service development.[14] First, bids were ranked on the basis of needs assessment, with the greatest weight being attached to services that met local needs. Then, following the preparation of a shortlist, the proposals were ranked using the following criteria:

- robustness or the extent to which the proposal can be implemented — 0–3
- promotion of equity — 0–1
- evidence of effectiveness or cost-effectiveness — 0–2
- collaboration or integration with primary care — 0–3
- prioritized by the community health council (a statutory body representing patients) — 0–1
- prioritized by local GPs — 0–1
- other possible or more appropriate sources of funding — 0–5 (negative score)

As can be seen, the greatest weight was attached to other funding methods, using a negative score as high as 5 to cancel out the other weightings. Since this system was first prepared, an age dimension has been added to consideration of effectiveness. Over the next few years, consideration will increasingly be given to benefit by age groups – children, adults and older people.

The scores were first determined by the Director of Public Health and then discussed by the purchasing team and members of the health authority. Although other authorities use different scoring methods, this process is fairly typical of the way in which development proposals are prioritized.

Novel methods employed at Southampton

Southampton found a way to take a more proactive stance and link the process more closely with purchasing decisions. It also gave the Commission's non-executive members room to exert greater influence over the process of selection.

Instead of waiting for bids to be presented by providers, the Commission developed a health strategy of its own. It broke down its total expenditure into eight disease-based programmes and identified 29 leading health problems. Assessments were then made of how to deal with them.

For example, with the programme on cancer, five types were identified as health problems: breast, lung, cervical, skin and bowel. To deal with them, four interventions were chosen: home-based palliative care, concentration of treatment in specialist teams, prevention of skin cancer and early recognition of skin lesions.

This exercise was repeated for all eight programmes and resulted in a total of 49 interventions needed to deal with the 29 health problems. These 49 became the options to be considered for expenditure of growth money. No shortlist was compiled by the Director of Public Health or the purchasing team; the non-executive members wanted the Commission to make the selection itself.

Setting criteria

The Commission then had to decide how the money would be spent. It did so first by selecting the criteria it would use and deciding the importance it would attach to each. Initially, five were chosen, with health gain and equity assuming the greatest weight.

However, before the process was completed, nine more were added, the most important being the extent to which options conformed to national initiatives. Even then, the rank order decided could not always be followed because consideration had to be given to factors such as previous commitments.

Too many options

The process turned out to be unduly complex. From this and other exercises, it is evident that not more than five or ten options can be considered at one time. In Southampton, this was eventually realized by making choices first by health programme, or what might be called 'bite-size chunks'. That procedure had been followed for several years but without adequate follow-through; too many choices had been allowed to lie on the table.

In addition, the 49 options could have been reduced by entrusting an initial selection to those who conduct the preliminary assessment of needs. In the UK, that task is carried out by public health personnel.

Conflict between national and local priorities

The experience also revealed the way in which national initiatives can distort local priorities. When the Commission had only its own criteria to consider, it assigned higher rankings to chronic and community care than to acute services in hospital, but when account had to be taken of national initiatives much higher rankings were given to those dealing with the acute sector, particularly one designed to reduce waiting time for elective surgery.

This conflict of priorities has yet to be resolved by the government. In the face of hospital closures and other cutbacks, health authorities generally are under pressure to shift resources in the community direction. Although the government strongly supports this trend, it continues to thwart attempts by issuing directives to cut waiting lists.

Public consultation

Much effort has gone into means of consulting the public, and this effort has been led by the Department of Health. A method first used asked the public to rank specific interventions in priority order, but it was found that relevant information had to be provided so that informed choices could be made. In one survey, intensive care for premature babies ranked highly in the pilot project, but the ranking dropped markedly when it was pointed out that 'babies weighing less than one and a half pounds are unlikely to survive'.[16] Similar findings emerged from another survey, with the rank order supplied by the public being less consistent than that given by better-informed doctors and managers.[17]

Even when supplied with relevant information, many people do not feel comfortable or competent to make rationing decisions, preferring to leave them to doctors. Doctors, however, do not want to bear the onus; they want a clear lead from the Department of Health. Despite this, no action has yet been taken, so rationing decisions remain in the hands of the managers and non-executive members who make up district health authorities. This has placed them in a difficult position when hard choices have to be made.

Need for public involvement

If such choices are to be accepted, then some public involvement is required, in both a proactive and reactive sense. The former seeks to elicit the values or ethical principles that should influence the way in which resources are distributed. Public meetings have been poorly attended, and a more promising method has been found in the form of focus groups.

Focus groups consist of 10 or 12 people constituting a representative sample of the local population. Views are exchanged in prolonged discussions and reflect the values held. In general, members of the public place great value on equity and feel that some consideration should be given to the way in which lifestyle affects the need for care. Those who ruin their health do not always win sympathy from the public.

The Somerset Health Authority has devised an effective method of using focus groups.[18] Eight groups, each consisting of 12 people, meet three times a year. They are asked about issues that concern the health authority as well as to score certain priorities. Background information is supplied and discussions are tape recorded. The views expressed have been found to be representative, valid and focused on community rather than individual values. They have thus influenced health authority decisions.

Public involvement is also needed in a reactive sense. This is achieved by exposing the process by which priorities are set to public view. Only in this way, it is felt, can difficulties be understood and confidence won. The main aim is to show the public that every effort has been made to reach fair and just decisions.

Community health councils are statutory bodies representing patients in each district, and some have actively participated in the consultation process. However, others have proved reluctant, fearful of being involved in an exercise that may impose restrictions on care.

GP fundholding

The UK is unique in having a corps of GPs who set their own priorities by holding budgets. At present, they are responsible for only about 30% of the care they provide, but experiments are under way to see whether they can handle it all.

This movement is being fostered with the strong support of the central government. It likes the way in which fundholding has extended the range of GP care and established closer links with the hospital world. Fundholding gives GPs more influence over the provision of specialist services; some outpatient clinics are now held in GP surgeries. Also, with their clinical expertise and close contact with patients, GPs are thought to be better able than health authorities to assess patient demands, set priorities and secure adequate specialist services. They are consulted more frequently than the public, and the priorities they choose – largely for acute services – are commonly reflected in purchasing plans.[11]

However, GP fundholding has been criticized by the Labour Party (the main opposition party), which would prefer to phase it out. The Party dislikes the two-tiered service that fundholding produces, with patients of fundholders receiving preferential treatment from the hospital world.

GPs are well placed to assess patient demands, but they find it difficult to assess needs. Their contact with patients is limited to those who *seek* care, not to those who may need it. Fundholders also cover too few patients for efficient purchasing; some conditions are rarely seen and too many contracts have to be negotiated, thereby producing high administrative costs.

The government likes GP fundholding because it provides a way to put cash limits on a service largely free from financial restraints. Labour, however, fears that the financial restraints may prove too strong and will induce GPs to withhold services from high-cost patients. The elderly and chronic sick are felt to be particularly at risk.

At the moment little is known about the way in which GPs set priorities, and studies are badly needed. But if fundholder preferences are like those of GPs generally, then the main concern is with problems arising from the acute sector, particularly long waiting times and access to certain specialties.[11]

These political differences might be resolved by the development of commissioning groups embracing all GPs. Some have already been formed, and it will be necessary to see if they can retain the benefits of fundholding without its disadvantages.

References

1 Effective Health Care Bulletin (1994) *Implementing Clinical Practice Guidelines*. Bulletin No. 8, University of Leeds, Leeds.
2 NHS Executive (1993) *Improving Clinical Effectiveness*. EL(93)115, NHS Executive, Leeds.
3 NHS Executive (1994) *Improving the Effectiveness of the NHS*. EL(94)74. NHS Executive, Leeds.
4 House of Commons Health Committee (1995) *Priority Setting in the NHS: Purchasing*. First Report, Session 1994–95, HC 134–1. Her Majesty's Stationery Office, London.
5 Department of Health (1995) *Government Response to the First Report for the Health Committee Session 1994–95*. Cmnd 2826. Her Majesty's Stationery Office, London.
6 Redmayne S (1995) *Reshaping the NHS – Strategies, Priorities and Resource Allocation*. National Association of Health Authorities and Trusts, Birmingham.
7 Honigsbaum F, assisted by Ham C (1996) *Improving Clinical Effectiveness: the Development of Clinical Guidelines in the West Midlands*. Health Services Management Centre, University of Birmingham.
8 Klein R (1993) Dimensions of rationing: who should do what? *BMJ* **307**: 309–311.
9 Ham C and Heginbotham C, with Cochrane M and Richards J (1992) *Purchasing Dilemmas*. King's Fund College, London.
10 Klein R and Redmayne S (1992) *Patterns of Priorities*. National Association of Health Authorities and Trusts, Birmingham.
11 Redmayne S, Klein R and Day P (1993) *Sharing out Resources – Purchasing & Priority Setting in the NHS*.

National Association of Health Authorities and Trusts, Birmingham.

12 Court C (1995) Survey shows widespread rationing in NHS. *BMJ* **311**: 1453–1454.

13 Jones G (1995) Dorrell warns health authorities against NHS 'rationing'. *Daily Telegraph*, 9 January, page 4.

14 Ham C, Honigsbaum F and Thompson D (1994) *Priority Setting for Health Gain*. Department of Health, London.

15 Honigsbaum F, Richards J and Lockett T (1995) *Priority Setting in Action*. Radcliffe Medical Press, Oxford.

16 Bowling A, Jacobson B and Southgate L (1993) Health Service priorities: explorations in consultation of the public and health professionals on priority setting in an inner London health district. *Social Science and Medicine* **37**: 851–857.

17 Heginbotham C (1993) Health care priority setting: a survey of doctors, managers and the general public. In: Smith R (ed) *Rationing in Action*. BMJ Publishing Group, London, pp. 141–156.

18 Bowie C, Richardson A and Sykes W (1995) Consulting the public about health service priorities. *BMJ* **311**: 1155–1158.

Part 2

Trends and issues

Trends and issues

From this review of priority setting developments a number of trends can be seen and they, in turn, give rise to issues that need to be resolved. This chapter explores both. They are listed first in summary form; then, each is discussed in turn.

Summary

- Priority setting processes are tending to rely increasingly on the use of clinical guidelines rather than the exclusion of services. Even Oregon has found it necessary to use guidelines to determine when exceptions are justified.
- Only in the UK has no national initiative been taken to debate or set principles for priorities; rather, targets are proposed for health authorities to meet and efforts are concentrated on the development of evidence-based medicine. However, The Netherlands is now moving in the direction of the UK, relying on the local adoption of clinical guidelines.

- Needs assessment has progressed furthest in UK. Elsewhere, except at the regional level in New Zealand, it has not received the same attention, and in Oregon it has been entirely neglected.
- Equity and health gain are emerging as the most important values considered in setting priorities. Rationing involves considerations of equity from the standpoint of individuals and minority groups, but as financial pressures increase more emphasis is being put on health gain for the population as a whole.
- There is no quick fix or clear way to apply values or set priorities. Subjective judgements are inevitably involved, but methods are being developed to secure consensus.
- An increasingly common way of setting priorities is by means of 'bite-size chunks', but this presents problems. For it to work, relevant information must be available, but that makes it easier to apply to acute rather than chronic conditions. Also, successful use depends on rapid implementation. If choices are allowed to lie on the table, then different methods are needed to set priorities, similar to those which apply to the whole of health care.
- No satisfactory method has been devised to determine how resources should be generally allocated between different services. Some method of programme budgeting and marginal analysis may offer a way forward, but the technique is at an early stage of development.
- Oregon has gone the furthest in excluding services, but few hard choices have been made there or elsewhere. Exclusions have generally lain on the margins of health care, ruling out services such as cosmetic surgery. However, there is a significant contrast in the treatment of dental services for adults: they are not publicly funded in New Zealand and The Netherlands, whereas Oregon covers all but tooth implants and bleaching.

- Generally, priorities have been set with the aim of shifting resources in the direction of prevention together with chronic and community care. However, progress has been slow and realization is doubtful if reliance is placed on clinical guidelines or waiting lists.
- Waiting lists for treatment offer a seductive means of setting priorities since simple statistical targets can be set in the form of maximum waiting times. They are also the subject of widespread public concern, which makes time limits popular with politicians. But these targets are concerned mainly with waits for elective surgery, which means that chronic conditions may be neglected, thereby producing an in-built bias towards the acute sector.
- Quality of life considerations have been ruled out in Oregon and are disliked in Sweden because they may discriminate against disabled and elderly persons. A different method is gaining favour which takes account of the views of disabled persons and years of lower, as well as those of higher, quality. It is called disability-adjusted life years (DALYs).
- Age and lifestyle *per se* have generally been ruled out as factors in setting priorities. They may be taken into account only when they are likely to affect the outcome of treatment. However, nowhere have procedures been devised to ensure that this distinction applies.
- Focus groups are being increasingly used as the most effective means of public consultation. Their main aim is to elicit the values that should determine priorities. Attempts to secure rankings for specific treatments may aid this process, but only if relevant information is provided. However, the public generally does not wish to make hard choices, preferring to leave those to the doctors.

- GP fundholding has taken root only in the UK, but its future is uncertain. If it develops very far, it will restrict the role of health authorities in the priority setting process. Other ways of involving GPs are being tried which leave scope for wider action and closer co-operation.
- More involvement by providers is needed if resources are to be allocated appropriately, but procedures have to be devised to ensure that this does not distort priorities. The most promising method is by means of budget-holding, covering not only GPs but specialists and other health personnel.
- Separate funding is needed for new treatments. Success rates for these may be low initially but often improve with time. Funding can best be handled on a national basis with treatment provided at highly specialized centres.

Clinical guidelines versus exclusions

Priority setting processes are tending to rely increasingly on the use of clinical guidelines rather than the exclusion of services.

Convergent to clinical guidelines rather than the exclusion of services. Oregon led the way in priority setting by excluding services, but its methods have not been taken up elsewhere, not even in the US. Interest, rather, has turned in the direction of more efficient operation and evidence-based medicine. Oregon itself has found it necessary to develop clinical guidelines to determine when exceptions should be made. They will also be used to determine when services should be withheld from those which are funded.

The Netherlands followed Oregon's lead by developing a funnel model that can be used to exclude services, but faced with stiff resistance in that direction it now sees clinical guidelines as the best way to push the process forward.

New Zealand has largely ruled out exclusions and is developing clinical guidelines to determine when services should be provided. However, it recognizes that it will not be possible to cover the whole of health care; effort is being concentrated on high-cost, high-volume procedures.

The UK has allowed exclusions to be made at the local level, but national effort is going into the development of evidence-based medicine and the use of clinical guidelines.

Sweden and Norway have not yet ruled out specific services, nor have they given much attention to the development of clinical guidelines. National effort, rather, has been directed at the development of priority setting principles and the reduction of waiting lists, decreasing the time before treatment is provided.

Outside of Oregon, there is thus a reluctance to exclude services except on the margins of health care. Politicians and the public alike find it more comfortable to stimulate the development of clinical guidelines. If sufficient funds are saved, then other measures may be delayed. However, in the face of the rising costs of health care and the financial pressures facing governments everywhere, more explicit forms of rationing may eventually have to be considered.

Need to define basic health care

If this involves the exclusion of services as Oregon has done, then attempts may have to be made to define a basic package of care. Oregon has thus far failed to do so, but with financial pressures mounting more lines are likely to be cut. If the plan is not to be discredited, some minimum point of provision will have to be set.

This will not be easy to do, and arbitrary decisions may have to be made. Because of the advance of medical science and the changing nature of clinical practice, definitions will have to be flexible, subject to periodic review. But if the process by which this is done is open to public view and seen to be fair, it may be accepted.

Payments by patients for excluded services

One way to limit access is to require payments by patients for services of dubious benefit when limited evidence of effectiveness is available, or when resources are not adequate to meet demand. Under this arrangement, basic services would be covered completely but others would not be completely excluded. The full cost would not be charged but their provision would depend on some contribution from patients in the form of initial charges or co-payments.

This might apply, for example, in the case of procedures such as *in vitro* fertilization or when patients seek services beyond those deemed appropriate by clinicians. Thus, endoscopy could be fully covered for patients with gastrointestinal bleeding, but payment would be required for an assessment of dyspepsia. This method has been suggested as a way of securing universal health care in the US[1] and resembles the techniques used in Europe, where more direct rationing techniques have been slow in forthcoming (e.g. France and Germany).

Advantages of guidelines

Meanwhile, reliance is increasingly being placed on guidelines, and the merits of this approach need to be compared with those of exclusions. Consideration also needs to be given to the way in which the two methods can be combined.

Exclusions are a blunt instrument; guidelines permit fine-tuning, enabling account to be taken of outcome as well as effectiveness before treatment is provided.

Guidelines also enable appropriate limits to be set in the way in which diagnoses are established. Where service exclusions are used, as in Oregon, no restrictions are placed on the number of investigations needed to assess the cause of illness. Everyone is entitled to a diagnosis and excessive tests may be employed.

Guidelines are more likely to win public acceptance, which makes the technique more attractive to politicians. Exclusions are generally resisted by the public and politicians are fearful of losing votes with this form of rationing. Oregon has thus far found acceptance of exclusions because its priority list applies only to the poor; if it were ever extended to a wider segment of the population, as originally intended, then more protests might be heard.

Disadvantages of guidelines

Guidelines are difficult and time-consuming to prepare, but even harder to implement. No effective strategy has yet been devised.

Guidelines are narrowly focused and cannot cover the whole of care, not even for many of the conditions for which they are designed. They offer no means of shifting resources across broad categories of care. Nor is there any certainty that they will cut costs; some, in fact, may raise them.

Guidelines may be subject to local variation so that the procedures offered varies from place to place or even from clinician to clinician. Much depends on the way in which they are applied and audited.

Guidelines put priority setting back in the hands of clinicians; although the process of preparation may be open to public view, clinicians decide when treatment will be provided. Their decisions may be influenced by the age, lifestyle or social situation *per se* of the patient concerned, not solely by the way in which these factors affect outcome. No procedures have yet been designed to avoid this possibility.

Advantages of exclusions

Exclusions may be decided through a public process and are easier to implement. Once set, they can be uniformly applied; only unjustified variations in diagnoses may alter the pattern. They also have an immediate effect on costs, reducing expenditure for the services excluded.

Disadvantages of exclusions

Exclusions are a blunt instrument; they deny treatment to patients who might receive sufficient benefit to justify provision.

Exclusions stir media interest and may arouse public protest; they are less likely to be accepted than guidelines. However, this may not apply where clinicians are concerned; some may prefer to have the decision to withhold treatment taken out of their hands so as to free themselves from the stigma.

Exclusions have limited application unless decisions are made arbitrarily; not enough data are available to cover the whole of health care, as was the case in Oregon. However, there may be situations in which exclusions are the only way to reduce costs and choices based on subjective judgements may have to be made. Limits also apply to the movement for evidence-based medicine or measures to provide care more efficiently.

There is no certainty that exclusions will shift resources in a desired direction. In Oregon, they were directed mainly at ineffective treatments or conditions on the margins of health care; few hard choices were made. So many acute conditions were funded that the chronic sector may have been somewhat neglected. This makes it doubtful whether Oregon will be able to achieve its aim of shifting resources towards prevention and community care.

How to combine guidelines with exclusions?

Guidelines may either precede or follow exclusions. If exclusions come first, then the public can be consulted in the process and the methods exposed to public view. Guidelines may then be developed to determine when exceptions may be made and a procedure established to subject the process to managerial review.

In the UK, this procedure already exists in the form of extracontractual referrals. Services normally provided are often arranged through block contracts, but when other care is sought (usually only available outside the district) then the clinicians involved must secure health authority approval. Expert specialist opinion must be sought and decisions made on a case-by-case basis. Charges or co-payments such as those described above are not imposed, but this is the point where they could most appropriately be applied.

If guidelines come first, then clinicians have greater freedom to decide when care is appropriate and treatment may be more quickly provided. The referral process described above takes time.

If treatment is provided, the patients involved will no doubt prefer this method, but the process will not be exposed to public view. Clinicians then make decisions on their own and may not always reveal the reason why care is being withheld. If a doctor says, 'I can do nothing more for you', how is the patient to know that is so?

Oregon is following the first method, New Zealand and the UK, the second, with The Netherlands about to follow suit. The guideline approach seems to be preferred wherever public resistance to exclusions is strong. This is more likely to apply where wide segments of the population are covered and a system of comprehensive provision has prevailed. Oregon, with its priority list confined to the poor, has thus far managed to avoid this reaction.

National or local discretion?

In the UK, priorities have been set in the form of targets on reducing specific health problems. They have been proposed on a national basis for district health authorities to reach, and much effort has gone into the development of evidence-based medicine. However, unlike experience elsewhere, no guidance has been given on the principles to follow and decisions are left to local discretion. However, The Netherlands is moving towards greater local discretion and, with its emphasis on clinical guidelines, New Zealand is heading the same way.

A movement for evidence-based medicine may have national direction and guidelines may be developed by national bodies, but implementation depends on the judgement of clinicians.

Priority setting based on guidelines thus inevitably involves local discretion, whereas exclusions may be decided either nationally or locally.

National direction may ensure uniform provision and avoid variations in service from locale to locale. It may relieve local managers of the need to make hard choices and avoid public protests due to geographical inequities. It may also free clinicians from the stigma associated with rationing decisions.

However, national direction may fail to take account of the need for local variations: some services may be required more than others. Targets set nationally (such as those on waiting lists) may also distort local priorities, frustrating attempts to shift care from the acute to the chronic sector.

Separate funding for new treatments

Although a trend towards local discretion seems to be under way, countervailing pressures may arise from the development of expensive, life-saving technologies. Variations in local provision may not be tolerated when lives are at stake.

New treatments thus present special problems. Until their worth is proven, the benefits may not be sufficient in relation to the risks and costs involved. Heart transplants are now successful, but not many patients survived when the first operations were performed.

When lives are at stake, this can present decision-makers as well as patients with difficult choices. With the rapid advance of medical science, more and more cases of this type are likely to appear, and they can probably best be handled on a national basis with treatment provided at highly specialized centres. Funding would come from the provision made for research and development. That might avoid the periodic controversy that arises with such cases whenever a local health authority finds it advisable to withhold treatment.

Needs assessment

Except in the UK and at the regional health authority level in New Zealand, needs assessment has been relatively neglected.

Before priorities are set, some assessment of needs, together with a stocktaking of existing services, seems essential, but only in the UK and New Zealand has this process taken hold. Oregon has completely neglected it, thereby failing to fund treatments which are urgently needed (as for obesity) despite some evidence of effectiveness. There, as elsewhere, policy-makers may not find it tenable to allow proof of effectiveness to override other considerations.

Needs assessment in the UK has been based mainly on broad epidemiological data, but more detail may be desirable to identify pockets of deprivation. The process also has to be linked more closely with purchasing decisions. Southampton found a way to do this by means of programme budgeting, and that method, together with marginal analysis, holds promise for the future.

Once the links are made, the options available for resource allocation need to be held to manageable numbers. Choices are difficult to make if more than ten or 12 are involved. To reduce the number, some method of short-listing may be required, which is best left to those who make the assessment of needs.

Equity and health gain

Equity and health gain are emerging as the most important values considered in setting priorities.

Rationing is essentially about equity, attempting to ensure that scarce resources are apportioned fairly. Where health care is concerned, this means paying attention to the demands of individuals and the needs of minority groups or those, such as the mentally ill, who find it difficult to speak for themselves.

Health gain is concerned with the extent to which benefits accrue to the population as a whole. It attempts to add life to years as well as years to life, and places the needs of the community first.

Equity is favoured by medical ethicists and philosophers, who are concerned with individual and minority rights. They see health in social terms and define disability widely, taking account of mental as well as physical effects. Strong support comes from the public, stemming from the belief that no one should be deprived of services they need.

Health gain is favoured by health economists, who stress the need for health authorities to live within budgets and provide the greatest good for the greatest number. Their approach is utilitarian and takes account of the costs associated with treatments as well as their clinical effectiveness.

Priority setting in Oregon arose out of a concern for equity; it aimed to provide care to all the poor, not just some. However, among the 13 values used to prepare the priority list in Oregon, equity was not rated highly. It was not considered essential to health care or even of value to society; its only importance was felt to be the individual needing the service. This reflects the weak concern for equity evident in the US generally; now that South Africa is starting a national health plan, the US is the only developed country without one.

Concern for equity appears to be strongly felt in Sweden, the UK and New Zealand, all countries with public systems that have long provided comprehensive care to the population as a whole. Once this benefit is held, the public is reluctant to accept restrictions no matter how pressing the need may be.

However, in all three countries, budgetary concerns are growing, and this is forcing greater attention to the costs of treatment, thereby placing increasing emphasis on health gain. That is likely to be the predominant value in setting priorities.

One way of reconciling the concepts of health gain and equity may be by allowing special funding for individual and minority needs. In the UK, this is provided by the process of extracontractual referrals, but treatment must be justified before approval is given.

Securing consensus

There is no clear way to apply values or set priorities; subjective judgements are inevitably involved but methods are being developed to secure consensus.

Values are easier to find than use; there is no clear way to apply them to the setting of priorities. Oregon elicited 13 values from community meetings, but they were classified and used in a subjective manner. To secure a consensus, a modified Delphi method was employed, which allowed scope for individual judgement and discussion.

Southampton tried different ways to relate criteria to options and produced conflicting results. In the end, a procedure was devised which allowed individual scores to be registered and then an average taken of the results. 'Gut feelings' may have exerted considerable influence.

One way of assessing criteria influence may be by means of a before-and-after method. At Southampton, Commission members were not asked to rank options before the discussion began. Had they done so, the order could have been compared with the ranks finally assigned.

No matter what method is used, judgements are involved and the most that can be expected is that they be as informed as possible.

Bite-size chunks

The most satisfactory way of setting priorities is by means of 'bite-size chunks' but this presents problems. Since more information is available for acute conditions, it focuses attention on them rather than the chronic sector. Also, too many choices may accumulate if they are not implemented when made.

Only Oregon has devised a method which sets priorities across the whole of health care but many find this method wanting because of data deficiencies. A reliable array of information is available only for identifiable groups of procedures or work which is discrete and can be handled separately within a workable timeframe.

The care of heart disease patients was the example used in the simulation seminar at Southampton in 1991 and, as with such care generally, it was found that more data were available with regard to treatment than to prevention and rehabilitation. Nevertheless, of the three methods tested, this 'bite-size chunk' approach was felt to be the most satisfactory way of setting priorities. Both there and in Stockholm, it was seen as the most hopeful way forward.

In both places, however, difficulties have arisen. Since data are more readily available for acute conditions, the chronic sector finds it hard to compete. Also, too many choices were allowed to lie on the table after the priority decisions were made, thereby making selection difficult when the time for implementation finally came.

These difficulties might be overcome in two ways:

1. The 'bite-size chunk' method could be retained where sufficient information is available, but measures are needed to ensure that choices are implemented once they are made.
2. Separate funding could be provided for the chronic sector by an overall allocation of resources, with proportions set by means of a procedure similar to that used for programme budgets in Southampton. Choices within the chronic sector would then be based on whatever information is available.

No satisfactory method

No satisfactory method has been devised to determine how resources should be generally allocated, but Southampton's system of programme budgeting may provide a way forward.

Only Oregon has set priorities across the whole of health care and, by classifying conditions within broad categories, it has attempted to determine the way in which funds should be generally allocated. Life-saving treatments with full recovery came at the top, followed by maternity, while procedures with little or no effect came at the bottom. However, so many changes were made by manual adjustments that category rankings may have significantly altered. Furthermore, because of a federal ruling, the category method had to be dropped.

A different way of allocating resources has been devised in Southampton. This makes use of programme budgets, with allocations based on assessments of relative priorities, distance from health targets, availability of effective interventions and efficiency of current resource use. A large element of subjective judgement goes into the process and, as many details have to be considered, the decisions may have to be made by those who examine them.

Other methods may be needed to supplement this process. At Southampton, the only attempt to set priorities was by programme, and that was done through the funding proportions assigned to each. The category classification used in Oregon had a more specific aim and grouped individual treatments together in priority order. Marginal analysis might be used for the same purpose. Adaptations of these methods are likely to be tested.

Exclusions

Oregon has gone the furthest in excluding services, and the recent cuts proposed mean that over one-fifth of the services on the priority list – 163 out of 744 – will not be publicly funded. However, although the denial of some services will cause concern, few hard choices have been made. Nevertheless, if financial pressures force further cuts, then treatment for serious conditions such as cancer of the gall bladder will be withdrawn.

Elsewhere also, few hard choices have been made. In the UK, they have involved mainly treatments of doubtful benefit; otherwise, exclusions have lain on the margins of health care, ruling out services such as cosmetic surgery.

However, there is a significant difference in the treatment of dental services: they are generally provided for children but not for adults in New Zealand or The Netherlands whereas Oregon offers adults all but tooth implants and bleaching. Although substantial charges for treatment are now imposed in the UK, they are still covered by the National Health Service.

This suggests that dental services for adults may come to be seen as a necessary provision only where access is limited to those who can pass means tests. Where whole populations are covered, there appears to be a feeling in two of the countries studied that dental services for adults can be left to individual responsibility. This view seems to be taking hold also in the UK.

Shifting resources to prevention and chronic and community care

Generally, priorities have been set with the aim of shifting resources in the direction of prevention together with chronic and community care. But progress has been slow, and realization is doubtful if reliance is placed on clinical guidelines and waiting lists.

Priority setting has to a large extent been inspired by a desire to shift resources to chronic and community care, but this is difficult to achieve unless models can be developed which cover the whole of health care.

The Netherlands, with its funnel procedure, has developed such a model with the explicit aim of aiding the chronic sector and vulnerable groups such as the mentally ill. However, this system has yet to come into operation, and effort is now being placed on the development of clinical guidelines.

Only Oregon has a model in operation which covers the whole of health care; procedures were formerly classified in categories which assigned higher rankings to prevention and some chronic conditions. However, list order was strongly influenced by data supporting treatment effectiveness, which can be seen more clearly in the acute sector. Furthermore, the category classification had to be abandoned because it was said to discriminate against disabled persons. Thereafter, so many manual adjustments were made that it is doubtful if funding will produce much of a shift towards chronic care.

Southampton, with its system of programme budgeting, appears to have developed a more reliable means of making such shifts. Of the eight programmes used, mental health received the largest share in the formula which set health strategy, and this priority is reflected in the purchasing plan finally produced. Not only was a mental health option selected as the first to be implemented, but six others from the programme – more than from any other programme – are likely to follow.

Only the need to meet national targets such as that on waiting lists produced distortions in priority towards the acute sector. Clinical guidelines have the same tendency as they are more applicable to acute than to chronic conditions.

Pressure from the acute sector

Generally, the public tends to favour the acute sector, particularly where life-saving treatments are involved, and specialists are adept at exploiting media pressure to secure support for expensive services.

Difficulties from this source may arise in Oregon as a result of the attempt to secure favourable treatment for mental health and chemical dependency services. These have been included in an integrated list with all but 12 of

49 items covered. Four more will be lost among the 27 additional lines to be cut, but that still leaves intact funding for 33 conditions, some of which can be extremely expensive to treat.

Schizophrenia, for example, is ranked as high as 159 out of 744 on the priority list, and a person suffering from this disorder will be entitled to a lifetime of care before a whole host of cancer sufferers are eligible for any form of treatment. If further funding pressure forces the cut-off point only 20 lines lower, no treatment would be provided for cancers of the oesophagus, liver, pancreas or gall bladder. That is likely to produce strong protests not only from patients afflicted with cancer and from oncologists, but also from the public at large.

Separate funding for the chronic sick

Protection for the chronic sick and vulnerable groups might be better provided through a system of separate funding, with priorities set by different methods from those used in the acute sector. Outcomes are more difficult to evaluate where chronic care is concerned, and high rankings for the mentally ill may be hard to justify if they are included in an integrated list such as the one in Oregon.

In many districts of the UK, mental health services are now provided through separate trusts. This ensures protection once funds are awarded, but the amounts allocated still depend on decisions made by purchasing authorities, and those will have to take account of both the need of the acute sector and the pressure specialists can mount. National agencies such as the Department of Health have greater freedom to act, and a system of separate funding may be needed before significant amounts can be shifted to prevention and care for the chronic sick.

In Sweden, the development has already been considered where prevention is concerned. The Priorities Commission raised the possibility of separate funding.

Waiting lists

Waiting lists offer a seductive means of setting priorities as simple statistical targets can be used but, because the procedure is concerned mainly with waits for elective surgery, it has an in-built bias towards the acute sector.

In Norway, priority setting procedures have focused on waiting lists, and Sweden has displayed a similar tendency. In the UK, national targets have also been set for waiting lists but, as the Southampton experience demonstrates, this can distort local priorities. The options dealing with waiting lists had to receive a much higher priority than the Southampton Commission desired, and the same applied to other options that dealt with the acute sector.

Public dissatisfaction runs high where waiting lists are concerned, and this makes the subject important to politicians. However, if local priorities are to prevail, separate funding for waiting list and similar targets are required.

Otherwise, administrative bodies need to be constructed so that they cover community as well as hospital care. In the UK, health commissions are being created for this purpose, and this will enable sufficient attention to be given to prevention together with chronic and community care.

In Norway, waits for treatment are deeply deplored, and similar feeling is evident in Sweden. However, if, as the Priorities Commission in Sweden desires, funding is to shift in favour of chronic care and vulnerable groups, a different focus may be needed.

QALYs versus DALYs

QALYs, or quality-adjusted life years, may one day be replaced by DALYs, or disability-adjusted life years.

Quality of life considerations have been ruled out of the priority setting procedure in Oregon and are losing favour in Sweden. A different method is developing, which takes account of the views of disabled persons and the benefit to be derived from a longer expectation of benefit despite some years of lower quality. The concept of quality-adjusted life years, or QALYs, may thus be replaced by one concerned with disability-adjusted life years, or DALYs.

In Oregon, quality of life considerations were rejected because they were held to discriminate against disabled persons under an Act passed in 1990. Criticisms were based on two counts: quality of life evaluations came from the general public, not disabled persons, and no account was taken of the benefit to be derived from years of lower quality. DALYs are designed to avoid both criticisms.

To take an example, if the general public thinks a procedure providing ten years of benefit will produce a quality of life of 50% of its expectations, then only five years would be considered in a QALY calculation. But those who have disabilities might assess the benefit differently and assess the quality of life at 70% of their expectations. Then an average would be taken of the two evaluations, or 60%, and that would mean that six instead of five years would be considered in a DALY calculation. Additional credit would be allowed for the final four years of lower quality.

Following this example through, if the procedure costs $1000 then the cost per year in a QALY calculation would be $200, but with a DALY it would be only $167, and that would be lowered further to take account of the final four years of lower quality. The procedure would thus be seen as more cost-effective with a DALY than with a QALY.

Although quality of life considerations were ruled out in Oregon, they are still used throughout the US in the development of clinical guidelines. However, the federal agency responsible – the Agency for Health Care Policy and Research – is conducting a project taking average quality of life scores on the DALY model. It remains to be seen whether this will be acceptable under federal law.

QALYs are not favoured in Sweden or New Zealand, but in the UK they are being developed with the active support of the Department of Health, and they are widely used elsewhere. Whether they should be replaced by DALYs is an issue that policy-makers will want to consider. Not all people react to disabilities in the same way and some – such as Christy Brown, the cerebral palsy sufferer depicted in the film *My Left Foot* – manage to live creative lives despite severe handicaps.

The World Bank, in conjunction with the World Health Organization, has developed a different method of calculating DALYs designed to estimate the burden of disease as well as the cost-effectiveness of interventions.[2] Their DALY takes account of the time lived with a disability as well as the time lost due to premature mortality, but it is based on the views of experts and not – directly at least – of disabled persons. Whether this will be acceptable under the Americans With Disabilities Act remains to be seen.

Age and lifestyle

Age and lifestyle factors are generally to be considered only in relation to an assessment of outcome, but nowhere have procedures been devised to ensure that this is so.

Age and lifestyle have generally been ruled out as criteria in setting priorities, but they may be considered by clinicians when assessing outcome. That puts discretion in the hands of clinicians and means that priorities could be set in the old implicit way.

In the UK, age has been a factor in determining access to renal dialysis, and it is explicitly recognized as such in New Zealand; there, patients over 75 will not normally be eligible for dialysis or kidney transplants. In the UK, smokers have been denied heart operations and it is not always clear that this has been done solely on the basis of an assessment of outcome.

Should age and lifestyle *per se* be considered as criteria for setting priorities? The need for care rises steadily as patients grow older and the elderly are forming larger proportions of the population everywhere. Some experts believe that age limits will one day have to be set. The leading exponent of this view is Daniel Callahan, Director of the Hastings Center in America. Many people feel that if hard choices have to be made, younger persons should be given preference. Those who have lived longer are felt to have had a 'fair innings' and the same possibility should be given to others.

As for lifestyle, some surveys of public opinion have found support for it to be considered as a factor in setting priorities. Only social factors – such as the extent to which the patient's work contributes to the community – may be an overriding consideration. Oregon, at one point, tried to deny liver transplants to alcoholics, but the proposal was withdrawn because it was seen as a form of discrimination against disabled persons.

Health systems everywhere are coming under funding pressure due to ageing populations, which means that not only age but also lifestyle and social factors may assume increasing importance in the way in which priorities are set.[3]

If age and lifestyle *per se* are not to be adopted as criteria, what measures can be taken to ensure that they are applied only in an assessment of outcome? An appeal procedure for patients, combined with an arrangement for second opinions, might be adequate. This is an issue of growing public concern and needs urgent attention.

Focus groups

Focus groups are increasingly being formed to elicit values that can be used in setting priorities, but members of the public generally do not want to make the hard choices, preferring to leave those to clinicians.

As a means of public consultation, community meetings have proved wanting. Few people attend, and in Oregon many who did were health service employees.

Attempts to have the public rank specific treatments have also had limitations. Relevant information has to be provided before informed judgements can be made and, even then, competence may be lacking. However, if the reasons for choices are sought, this method may be used to elicit the values or criteria the public would favour for priority setting.

Focus groups containing ten or 12 people are increasingly being employed as a means of consulting the public. If care is taken to ensure a fair representation of the local population, then relevant values may be elicited. Through discussion and exchange of views, participants can decide the criteria that they feel should be used in setting priorities.

However, members of the public generally have indicated that they do not wish to make the hard choices, preferring to leave those to clinicians. Clinicians, in turn, are increasingly reluctant to bear the burden and seek guidance from managers and/or politicians. How this guidance can best be supplied is another issue that needs urgent attention.

GP fundholding

GP fundholding has taken root only in the UK but, if it develops very far, it will restrict the role of health authorities in the priority setting process. Other means of involving GPs that are being tested leave scope for wider action by health authorities and closer co-operation with all GPs, not just fundholders.

GP fundholding has been unique to the UK, but it is starting in New Zealand and may be adopted elsewhere. It holds out the prospect of wider GP care and a closer tie with hospital services. With their medical expertise and intimate involvement with patients, GPs are well placed to set priorities and assess the services provided by specialists.

However, GP fundholders only see the patients who consult them and thus find it difficult to assess the wider needs of the community. The limited scope of their work also makes them unsuitable for planning strategic development and determining when local hospital services require protection from the pressures of an internal market. The special hospital attention their patients receive has created a two-tier service and produced strong protests from non-fundholding GPs. Of even greater concern may be the extent to which the financial pressures under which they operate may cause them to deny services to high-cost patients.

No one knows how fundholding GPs actually set priorities, but they make decisions in the old implicit manner, with choices not subject to public view as is the case with health authorities. For the most part, not even the patients of GPs seem to be involved in the process.

Different methods are being tried to involve all GPs in a joint advisory capacity, leaving health authorities free to set priorities and plan strategic development. Whether this will result in the loss of the benefits derived from fund-holding is uncertain. The main question involves the extent to which financial incentives to extend the range of care can be retained without producing harm to high-cost patients.

Involvement by providers

More involvement by providers is needed to allocate resources appropriately but procedures are required to ensure that this does not distort priorities.

Providers have thus far had only a small part to play in the setting of priorities. Their influence has been most evident in the UK, where they are consulted on the development of health strategy and present bids for growth money.

In many districts, providers also have the right to shift resources within block contracts, this discretion being usually limited to not more than 10% of the money involved. This can put some services at risk if funds are needed to cover deficits elsewhere. Thus, in one district where pressure was building in the acute sector, funds for chronic and community care had to be ring-fenced to protect these services.

Providers are normally consulted in the development of health strategy but their proposals are usually presented in the form of business plans, which can complicate matters.

In an attempt to simplify the way in which priorities are set in Southampton, providers will in future have to show how their proposals will contribute to health gain.

When it comes to the point where priorities are actually being decided, difficulties arise. Provider help is needed, but their participation can distort priorities. In one district, criteria were set by core group teams that included public and provider representatives as well as purchasers. But it is feared that this may distort priorities.

Those providing services in the acute sector have in the past exerted most influence and, where lives are at stake, the public is likely to support them. If chronic and community care are to receive their fair share of resources, then some form of programme budgeting may be needed before specific priorities are decided. And if providers actively participate in the decision-making process, then care must be taken to see that all the services under consideration are adequately represented.

How providers can most effectively be used presents a major challenge for the future. The most radical method under consideration is to let providers themselves set priorities within the framework of fixed budgets. Only the total amount allocated would be decided by purchasers, and that might be done by a method such as the one used in Southampton.

GP fundholders in the UK already operate under this principle, although they act as purchasers as well as providers. The method could be extended to hospital-based specialists through budgets assigned to specialty departments, and this procedure may soon be tested with clinical directorates in the UK.

Funding for new treatments

Separate funding for new treatments is discussed above in the section dealing with the movement away from national direction in setting priorities.

References

1 Stevens C D (1994) Correspondence on the case for the Clinton Plan of Health Reform. *New England Journal of Medicine* **330**: 1086–1087.
2 Murray C J L and Lopez A D (eds) (1994) *Global Comparative Assessments in the Health Sector.* World Health Organization, Geneva.
3 Callahan D (1987) *Setting Limits – Medical Goals in an Aging Society.* Simon & Schuster, New York.

Conclusion

Priority setting is so difficult that some despair of attempts to develop rational procedures and would let purchasers 'muddle through elegantly'.[1] Others would abandon the effort altogether and let priorities be set by clinicians in the same way as they did in the past.[2] For them, private procedures are preferable to public ones and they would be content to have priorities set once again behind closed doors.

Although members of the public prefer hard choices to be made by clinicians, they are not likely to tolerate the implicit methods used in the past. Expectations are rising, and if funding pressures force increasing restrictions on services the public will want to know how priorities are set.

The process, it is clear, cannot develop along completely rational lines; there are limits to the data that can be collected and subjective judgements will have to be made. The most that can be hoped is that it will be done in a way that will be seen to be fair.

That can best be achieved if methods are kept as simple as possible so that they can be understood. This may require greater reliance on the judgement of experts to prepare proposals so that informed choices can be made. A striving for simplicity is likely to be a key aim in the years ahead.

References

1 Hunter D (1993) *Rationing Dilemmas in Healthcare*. National Association of Health Authorities and Trusts, Birmingham.
2 Mechanic D (1995) Dilemmas in rationing health care services: the case of implicit rationing. *BMJ* **310**: 1655–1659.

Further reading

General

Ham C (1995) Synthesis: what can we learn from international experience? *British Medical Bulletin* **51**: 819–830.

Honigsbaum F, Calltorp J, Ham C and Holmström S (1995) *Priority Setting Processes for Healthcare*. Radcliffe Medical Press, Oxford.

Oregon

Castanares T (1995) *An Update on Priority-Setting in Oregon*. Paper presented to seminar, May 18–19. Health Services Management Centre, University of Birmingham, Birmingham.

Fox D M and Leichter H M (1991) Rationing Care in Oregon: the new accountability. *Health Affairs* (Summer): 7–27.

Fox D M and Leichter H M (1995) The ups and downs of Oregon's rationing plan. *Health Affairs* (Summer): 66–70.

Garland M J, Anderson B F and McNeil P A (1994) *Common Purpose in Health Policy*. Report of Focus Group Meetings. Oregon Health Decisions, Portland.

Honigsbaum F (1991) *Who Shall Live? Who Shall Die? Oregon's Health Financing Proposals*. King's Fund College Papers, London.

Kaplan R M (1994) Value judgment in the Oregon Medicaid experiment. *Medical Care* **32**: 975–988.

Kitzhaber J and Kenny A M (1995) On the Oregon trail. *British Medical Bulletin* **51**: 808–818.

Oregon Health Services Commission (1991) *Prioritization of Health Services*. A Report to the Governor and Legislature. Oregon Health Services Commission, Portland.

Oregon Health Services Commission (1995) *Prioritization of Health Services*. A Report to the Governor and Legislature. Oregon Health Services Commission, Portland.

Sipes-Metzler P (1994) Oregon Health Plan: ration or reason. *Journal of Medicine and Philosophy* **19**: 305–314.

US Congress, Office of Technology Assessment (1992) *Evaluation of the Oregon Medicaid Proposal*. OTA–H–532. Washington, DC, US Government Printing Office.

New Zealand

Ashton T (1993) From evolution to revolution: restructuring the New Zealand health system. *Health Care Analysis* **1**: 57–62.

Cooper M H (1995) Core services and the New Zealand health reforms. *British Medical Bulletin* **51**: 799–807.

Cumming J (1994) Core services and priority-setting: the New Zealand Experience. *Health Policy* **29**: 41–60.

Edgar W (1995) *Health Care Priority Setting in New Zealand.* Paper presented to seminar, May 18–19, Health Services Management Centre, University of Birmingham, Birmingham.

National Advisory Committee on Core Health and Disability Support Services (1992) *Core Services for 1993/1994.* Wellington.

National Advisory Committee on Core Health and Disability Support Services (1993a) *Core Services for 1994/1995.* Wellington.

National Advisory Committee on Core Health and Disability Support Services (1993b) *Ethical Issues on Defining Core Services.* A discussion document. Wellington.

National Advisory Committee on Core Health and Disability Support Services (1993c) *Seeking Consensus.* A discussion document. Wellington.

National Advisory Committee on Core Health and Disability Support Services (1993d) *The Best of Health 2. How We Decide on the Health and Disability Support Services We Value Most.* Wellington.

National Advisory Committee on Core Health and Disability Support Services (1994) *Core Services for 1995/6.* Wellington.

National Advisory Committee on Core Health and Disability Support Services (1995) *The Core Debater.* Issue No. 4, February. Wellington.

The Netherlands

Dunning Committee (1992) *Choices in Health Care*. A Report by the Government Committee on Choices in Health Care. Rijswijk.

Mulder J H (1995) *Priority Setting in Health Care: the Dutch Experience*. Paper presented to seminar, May 18–19, Health Services Management Centre, University of Birmingham, Birmingham.

Sheldon T (1994a) Dutch health reforms have failed, say ministers. *BMJ* **308**: 936.

Sheldon T (1994b) New Dutch health minister will need to compromise. *BMJ* **309**: 560–561.

Spanjer M (1995) Changes in Dutch health-care. *Lancet* **345**: 50–51.

ten Have H A M J (1993) Choosing Core Health Services in The Netherlands. *Health Care Analysis* **1**: 43–47.

van Willigenburg T (1993) Communitarian illusions: or why the Dutch proposal for setting priorities in health care must fail. *Health Care Analysis* **1**: 49–52.

Zwart H (1993) Rationing in The Netherlands: The Liberal and the Communitarian Perspective. *Health Care Analysis* **1**: 53–56.

Norway

Hansson L F, Norheim O F and Ruyter K W (1994) Equality, explicitness, severity, and rigidity: the Oregon Plan evaluated from a Scandinavian perspective. *Journal of Medicine and Philosophy* **19**: 343–366.

Nord E (1993) Unjustified use of the quality of well-being scale in priority setting in Oregon. *Health Policy* **24**: 45–53.

Norway's Public Inquiry (1987) *Guidelines for Priority Setting Within the Norwegian Health Care System*. Available only in the Norwegian language under reference, Norges offentlige utredninger NOU 23. Universitetsforlaget, Oslo.

Rolstad K (1995) *The Norwegian Experience*. Paper presented to seminar, May 18–19, Health Services Management Centre, University of Birmingham, Birmingham.

Sweden

Calltorp J (1989) The 'Swedish model' under pressure – how to maintain equity and develop quality? *Quality Assurance in Healthcare* **1**: 13–22.

Calltorp J (1990) Physician manpower politics in Sweden. *Health Policy* **15**: 105–118.

Calltorp J (1995) Sweden: no easy choices. *British Medical Bulletin* **51**: 791–798.

Holmström S (1995) *Sweden and Priority Setting*. Paper presented to seminar, May 18–19, Health Services Management Centre, University of Birmingham, Birmingham.

Swedish Parliamentary Priorities Commission (1993) *No easy choices – the Difficult Priorities of Healthcare*. Interim report, Ministry of Health and Social Affairs, SOU 5, Stockholm.

Swedish Parliamentary Priorities Commission (1995) *Priorities in Health Care*. Final report, Ministry of Health and Social Affairs, SOU 5, Stockholm.

United Kingdom

Bottomley V (1993) Priority Setting in the NHS. In: Smith R (ed) *Rationing in Action*. BMJ Publishing Group, London.

Bowie C, Richardson A and Sykes W (1995) Consulting the public about health service priorities. *BMJ* **311**: 1155–1158.

Cohen D (1994) Marginal analysis in practice: an alternative to needs assessment. *BMJ* **309**: 781–785.

Department of Health (1995) *Government Response to the First Report for the Health Committee Session 1994–95*. Cmnd 2826. Her Majesty's Stationery Office, London.

Glennerster H, Matsaganis M and Owens P (1994) *Implementing GP Fundholding: Wild Card or Winning Hand?* Open University Press, Buckingham.

Ham C (1995) *The UK Experience*. Paper presented to seminar, May 18–19, Health Services Management Centre, University of Birmingham, Birmingham.

Ham C and Heginbotham C with Cochrane M and Richards J (1992) *Purchasing Dilemmas*. King's Fund College, London.

Ham C and Shapiro J (1995) The future of fundholding. *BMJ* **310**: 1150–1151.

Ham C, Honigsbaum F and Thompson D (1994) *Priority Setting for Health Gain*. Department of Health, London.

Honigsbaum F, assisted by Ham C (1996) *Improving Clinical Effectiveness: the Development of Clinical Guidelines in the West Midlands*. Health Services Management Centre, University of Birmingham, Birmingham.

Honigsbaum F, Richards J and Lockett T (1995) *Priority Setting in Action – Purchasing Dilemmas*. Radcliffe Medical Press, Oxford.

House of Commons Health Committee (1995) *Priority Setting in the NHS: Purchasing*. First Report, Session 1994–95, HC 134–I, Her Majesty's Stationery Office, London.

Hunter D (1993) *Rationing Dilemmas in Healthcare*. National Association of Health Authorities and Trusts, Birmingham.

Klein R (1991) On the Oregon trail: rationing Healthcare. *BMJ* **302**: 1–2.

Klein R (1992) Warning signals from Oregon. *BMJ* **309**: 1457–1458.

Klein R (1993) Dimensions of rationing: who should do what? *BMJ* **307**: 309–311.

Klein R and Redmayne S (1992) *Patterns of Priorities*. National Association of Health Authorities and Trusts, Birmingham.

Mooney G, Gerard K, Donaldson C and Farrar S (1992) *Priority Setting in Purchasing*. National Association of Health Authorities and Trusts, Birmingham.

Petchey R (1995) General practitioner fundholding: weighing the evidence. *Lancet* **346**: 1139–1142.

Redmayne S (1995) *Reshaping the NHS – Strategies, Priorities and Resource Allocation*. National Association of Health Authorities and Trusts, Birmingham.

Redmayne S, Klein R and Day P (1993) *Sharing out Resources – Purchasing & Priority Setting in the NHS*. National Association of Health Authorities and Trusts, Birmingham.

Index